ENDORSE[illegible]

“Paul Johansson taps into the inc[illegible]g, boldness—producing power of the Gospel of Jesus Christ. As he unfolds the courtroom scene described in the Book of Romans, we finally hear clearly, ‘If God is for us, who can be against us?’ I encourage you to let the insights of this book to break the grip of condemnation in your life.”

MIKE CAVANAUGH,
President, Elim Bible Institute

“Through his right spiritual experience and prophetic insights, Paul Johansson masterfully unlocks secrets from the Apostle Paul’s letter to the Roman Church. After reading *Free by Divine Decree* you will feel as though the Apostle Paul was writing the letter directly to you.”

DR. DAVID IRELAND, PHD,
Senior Pastor, Christ Church, Montclair, new Jersey

“*Free by Divine Decree* makes Romans come alive, unlike any other book I’ve read on the subject. Paul clearly defines the liberating message of the freedom we have in Christ that frees us from guilt and condemnation. It’s a must read for any student of the Bible.”

DR. RON BURGIO,
President, Elim Fellowship, Lancaster, New York

“For years I have listened to Paul Johansson teach the Book of Romans and I think of him as ‘Mr. Romans.’ The writer of Romans makes our freedom a legal transaction. The metaphor used in this book is of an accused person sitting in courtroom with God the Father as judge at his criminal trial. *Free by Divine Decree* is a must for every believer. It is not only to be read, but to be experienced.”

BISHOP TOMMY REID,
Full Gospel Tabernacle, Orchard park, New York

"I took Paul Johansson's class on Romans at Elim Bible Institute 30 years ago, and it was truly life-transforming for me. The judicial drama of the book unfolded before my eyes. Years later, like well-aged wine, Paul has finally reduced the wealth of his understanding of Romans to book. What a gold mine! This book will serve anyone who is preaching, teaching, or studying the Book of Romans."

BOB SORGE,
Author, "Oasis House"

"A 21st century Apostle Paul brings to life the epistle to the Romans in Free by Divine Decree. The accuser condemned—our Advocate triumphantly victorious—cellar dwellers discover the height and price of Christ's outrageous grace. Intensely brilliant is the forum of the courtroom drama unveiling the prophetic parallels of freedom prescribed for yet another generation. A just read for both scholar and seeker."

NANCY CLARK,
President, Evangelical Women Leaders of the National Association of Evangelicals

"The courtroom setting in *Free by Divine Decree* provides an dearly demonstration of how the laws and covenants of God's Kingdom are applied in the courtroom of Heaven. Not only will this book free the reader from the guilt of sin, he/she will also gain a deep revelation of the character of God and the love mercy and justice. He makes available to all mankind."

CLARENCE "BUZ" SAWYERS,
Director of Publications, Business Men's Fellowship

"More than a handbook on Romans, *Free by Divine Decree* is the heartbeat of two authors, both named Paul. Paul Johansson has found the pulse of Paul the Apostle! Both hearts beat to proclaim the life-changing power of the Gospel. Building the case from the Apostle Paul's arguments, the present writer documents the legal process of our redemption as though it had been transacted in a heavenly courtroom.

REV. SYLVIA R. EVANS,
Founder, Creative Word Ministries

"Paul Johansson's years of missionary ministry, urban evangelism and classroom exposure are reflected in his handling of the Apostle Paul's letter to the Church in first century Rome. The letter is old, the problems have not changed and the answers need to be understood and applied as urgently now as they were when first written. This book is birthed in the writer's heart and mind as it was in the heart of the Apostle."

REV. DAVID EDWARDS,
President Emeritus, Elim Bible Institute

FREE BY DIVINE DECREE

Living Free of Guilt and Condemnation

The Book of Romans made practical

PAUL JOHANSSON

M·J

NASHVILLE

NEW YORK • LONDON • MELBOURNE • VANCOUVER

FREE BY DIVINE DECREE

Living Free of Guilt and Condemnation

The Book of Romans made practical

Published in New York, New York, by Morgan James Publishing. Morgan James is a trademark of Morgan James, LLC. www.MorganJamesPublishing.com

Proudly distributed by Ingram Publisher Services.

ISBN 9781614483700 paperback
ISBN 9781614483717 ebook
Library of Congress Control Number: 2012948204

Cover and Interior Design by:
David Danglis

Foreword		ix
Preface		xi
Acknowledgments		xiii
	ROMANS 1.1-17	
Part I	**Introduction**	**1**
Chapter 1:	A Legal Transaction	7
Chapter 2:	Key to Romans: Righteousness	11
Part II	**Courtroom: Prosecution's Evidence**	**15**
Chapter 3:	Present in the Courtroom: Servant, Savior, Saints, and Sinners	17
Chapter 4:	How Bad Is the Evidence?	25
	ROMANS 1.18-3.20	
Chapter 5:	The "Gross" Sinner	31
Chapter 6:	The "Good" Sinner	39
Chapter 7:	The "Religious" Sinner	45
Chapter 8:	Three Witnesses	55
	ROMANS 3.21-26	
Part III	**A Surprising Turn of Events**	**59**
Chapter 9:	Righteousness Apart from the Law	61
Chapter 10:	Courtroom Righteousness	65
Part IV	**The Believer's Defense Continues**	**77**
Chapter 11:	Courtroom: New Evidence	79
Chapter 12:	Courtroom: Righteousness by Faith Is True to History	87
	ROMANS 4-8	
Chapter 13:	Inheritance by Faith	95
Chapter 14:	The Nature of Abraham's Faith	99
Chapter 15:	God's Forgiveness through Jesus Christ	107
Chapter 16:	Justified	115
Chapter 17:	Reigning in Christ	125

Chapter 18:	The Believer's Relationship to Sin	127
Chapter 19:	Union with God	137
Chapter 20:	Courtroom: Legally Free from the Law	145
Chapter 21:	Life in Union with the Holy Spirit	155
Chapter 22:	The Godhead in Unity for Our Freedom: Not Guilty! Case Closed	165
	ROMANS 9-11	
Part V	**The Sovereignty of God**	**177**
Chapter 23:	God's Chosen People	179
Chapter 24:	Christian Consecration	189
Chapter 25:	Gifts of the Spirit	195
	ROMANS 12-15	
Part VI	**The "Not Guilty" Are Now Free to Serve**	**205**
Chapter 26:	Love is a Fruit	207
Chapter 27:	Subject to Governing Authorities	213
Chapter 28:	Scruples	221
Chapter 29:	Evangelism and Missions	233
	ROMANS 16	
Part VII	**Farewell**	**239**
Chapter 30:	Safeguards	241
Chapter 31:	Faith Powers Us Forward	245
Appendix 1:	Purpose and History	249
Appendix 2:	Outline	255
Appendix 3:	The Romans "Tree of Salvation"	257
Works Consulted		265

FOREWORD

Without a proper understanding of the book of Romans it is almost impossible for a believer to grow and mature in their Christian walk. This masterful theological treatise written by the Apostle Paul to the church at Rome rightly holds a unique place in all of Scripture. Reverend Paul Johansson is a minister with many gifts but his ability to teach Romans seems to be a special grace given by God. His regular expository lectures through the years at The Brooklyn Tabernacle proved not only a phenomenal blessing to thousands of students but were also instrumental in preparing numerous believers for their future placement in Christian ministry.

I am so happy that God has permitted Paul Johansson to write *Free By Divine Decree* so that vast numbers of people can now be enriched by his exposition of Romans. May God use this volume to strengthen the Body of Christ and bring more glory to God who gave His Son so that we might be free!

— Jim Cymbala

Senior Pastor, The Brooklyn Tabernacle

PREFACE

As a small stream begins to flow through a narrow gorge, over time it continues to widen and deepen the river bed. Through the years, many rich mineral deposits are added to the ever-increasing flow.

Similarly, when I first began to teach the book of Romans, a small trickle of life ran down to my students as I endeavored to use Romans to build a strong doctrinal understanding in their lives. In both Kenya and the United States, I had opportunities to pour this teaching of divine grace as a concrete foundation for true Christian living. In Kenya particularly, the solid Romans teaching has grounded hundreds of pastors and churches in the Word of God.

The Holy Spirit continued to hone the message as I taught students over many years at Elim Bible Institute. The flow and sharpening increased to meet the challenges of the 1960s and 1970s. Teaching in several great churches in New York City in the 1980s encouraged students to focus on the North Star of God's love, grace, and liberty as expressed in the book of Romans.

I discovered that many students (some even raised in church) did not have a solid understanding of the liberating message of Romans due to difficult cultural and/or urban pressures. These students' salvation seemed to hinge on good works as they struggled to live victoriously. It was pure joy for me to declare to them the inspired revelation as it is recorded in this volume: *Free by Divine Decree.* As my students sat quietly in the classroom listening to the truth of what Christ did for them, slowly the truth would dawn upon them and tears would flow down their faces as darkness turned to light. The message was getting through.

At the New York School of Urban Ministry, which my wife and I founded in 1984, I was able to strengthen and sharpen the focus of this book to highlight the courtroom scene used as the template. Before this time I had centered the teaching on the tree diagram located in Appendix 3 of this book. My goal was to emphasize that the life of the tree comes from the roots of chapters 4 through 8. As a believer abides in the root, the fruit of chapter 12 through 15 will blossom forth. The courtroom metaphor for me sharpened the divide between the vices and pressures of life in the city and the freedom of His spacious grace. Light was contrasted with darkness, grace with Law, and God's free gift with human effort.

Free by Divine Decree is written to bring you into a new freedom in Christ Jesus and to awaken a desire for a more thorough in-depth study of Romans and the sixty-five books that surround it.

The penalty of sin has been fully paid by Christ's sacrifice, and believers declared legally free are righteous. They are able now to walk in confidence and freedom.

Welcome into the divine courtroom. Keep your Bible handy. Have a seat. All quiet. The case is about to begin.

ACKNOWLEDGMENTS

Many wonderful people have invested heavily in my personal spiritual journey and have encouraged me to write. Now is the season, and I am inwardly compelled to give a return on their investment.

I acknowledge the rich deposit I received in my upbringing in a Christian family that had a heart for missions. My grandfather, Evan S. Williams, pioneered and pastored a church in New York City presently called Evangel Church and pastored by my brother Robert. Our parents took us to church and modeled the Christian life at home.

The following are those who have been directly involved in producing *Free by Divine Decree:*

My pastor at Elim Gospel Church, Mike Cavanaugh, continuously gave encouragement to facilitate this book. He was able to contact Randy Johnson, who recommended the help of typist Claire Rickard, who typed the first manuscript directly from my classroom tapes. This put the message in print, but required many hours of rehashing to get it to flow seamlessly.

This undertaking was embraced by Jodi Hokenson, wife of Pastor Jeff Hokenson of Arcade, New York. Without her continued commitment, this book would not have had the momentum to climb some of the uphill challenges we faced. She served foremost as copyeditor. Thank you, Jodi!

As the book proceeded, I felt it was necessary to have three others read some of the earlier manuscripts for comments from their areas of expertise. Because it is written in a judicial manner, thanks go to Mr. Mark Marquardt, a lawyer in Clearwater, Florida. His comments were very helpful. For a theological perspective, my friend, colleague, and Bible scholar at Elim Bible Institute, Rev. David Edwards, gave valuable insight. Thanks to Mrs. Mary Tatem, a published author in Virginia, for her succinct commentary on its readability and organization. Thanks to longtime personal friend Bob Sorge, author of a number of books, for his behind-the-scenes counsel and willingness to publish it by his Oasis House.

Words are inadequate to express my deep appreciation to my precious wife, Gloria, for her dedicated life and commitment to her Lord and then to me. We have grown together with over 50 years of marriage. She rose to this challenge as always and spent hours in typing and re-typing. The editing process has helped make the message clearer, but demanded many hours on the computer. At times we had to stop just to enjoy the fragrance of freedom's sacrifice.

There is a great cloud of students presently ministering worldwide who have drawn deeply from the fountain of Romans, and as they did, it deepened my own understanding and allowed the Spirit to season this whole book with His outrageous grace.

PART I

INTRODUCTION

Riding my motorcycle down a lonely trail in Masaai country Kenya, East Africa, I passed among fields full of beautiful zebras and light-footed impalas. I was returning from a church planting and was unaware of the huge ditch obscured by brush along the right-hand side of the road. This ditch measured six feet wide, six feet deep, and several miles long. It had been dug years earlier to stop elephants from crossing over from the game reserve into the villages.

I was traveling along well until I hit a muddy spot on the trail, which flipped me upside down and left me dangling from a low hanging branch positioned over the elephant ditch. As I hung upside down, my forehead sizzled on the cycle's exhaust. I fought my way off of the tree branch and into the ditch. Stunned and confused, I awakened to the sight of two Masaai women tilling their gardens. I called out to the women for help and soon we pulled the muddy motorcycle out of the ditch before pushing to get it started. I knew right away I would need healing from my injuries.

Along the path of each of our lives, there are many hidden dangers when we slip off the designated road. Usually, we remain unaware of the pitfalls until we go a different way and find ourselves in the "elephant ditch." Romans immediately describes the pit we were in, the off-road dangers, and the effects of the resulting injuries. It continues on to reveal a personal Savior full of protection and benefits for those who cry out for help. Christ places us on His trail and takes us straight away from the miry pit. This Savior sets us free from guilt and fills us with faith to travel on. He then gives us a personal "travel guide" by the name of the Holy Spirit who leads us and holds us on-course. Now, nothing "else in all creation, will be able to separate us from the love of God that is in Christ Jesus our Lord" (*NIV,* Rom. 8.39b).

Do you find yourself struggling with sin and condemnation? Do you desire instead to enjoy the overabundance of God's grace you are receiving? Do you feel like a failure when you don't live up to God's good requirements? Would you rather know you are a success story apart from measuring up to human assessments? Then this book of God's transforming grace is for you! You are invited to learn of what God has done for you as revealed in the transforming book of Romans. God has forgiven you. The love of God does not forgive you; the justice of God forgives you. He died for you because He loves you. Through His death, you are justified. God would be unjust not to forgive you when the price for your salvation has been paid in full by Jesus Christ. Romans is the book for understanding the basic foundation of this super salvation.

Romans is a book for the whole person. It deals with your body, your soul, and your spirit. In this commentary on the book of Romans, every area of your life will be touched. Nothing will be untouched because, although Paul authored the book, the Holy Spirit inspired it before it was delivered, most likely, by the hand of a faithful believer named Phoebe.

A LEGAL JUSTIFICATION

The book of Romans calls you to enter not a ballroom, but a courtroom. Whether or not you are justified before God in His courtroom depends not on your feelings, but rather on the fact that the eternal Judge of the universe has pronounced you "Not guilty." It is a logical conclusion, therefore, that what you do is not what justifies you; but rather what the Judge decrees is what justifies you. The issue of your salvation is not dependent on how you feel; it is dependent on what the just Judge declares based on the evidence.

How many days do you and I wake up to a "blue Monday" or a "blue week?" We are in the pits because we feel God, Satan, ourselves, or others may hold something we have done against us. We cannot seem to comprehend the word "breakthrough." What we can comprehend is that the heavens are as brass. You might say to yourself, "Well, I had a really bad day, but I'm praying and fasting." Praying and fasting are good and right, but the victory is gained first by believing. There are certain things that come forth by adding prayer and fasting; everything good comes forth by believing. Someone might argue that if a person has a drinking problem, it is prayer and fasting that will conquer that problem! Not true. Belief conquers problems. Victorious actions only follow right beliefs. Only believing will give the strength to embrace the truth.

LOOK FOR GOD TO FREE AND RELEASE YOU TO BE ALL THAT HE WANTS YOU TO BE, AND THEN TO PLACE YOU IN A SETTING WHERE YOU CAN BE YOURSELF IN SERVICE TO HIM.

The book of Romans is fully understood only by revelation. It is a revelation that will dawn on you. We may have built a system of beliefs that requires us to earn our salvation. Some people may mistakenly think that serving God well will earn a way to heaven. No deeds can purchase our salvation. It costs too much. It cost Jesus Christ His life. Only Jesus Christ was able to afford to pre-pay the full extravagant price of our salvation with His perfect sacrificial death. His payment was the final evidence that the Judge of all mankind needed to declare you and me, "Free, by divine decree."

May the release of the Holy Spirit be real in your life. May He free you in every way in your body, soul, and spirit. Look for God to free and release you to be all that He wants you to be, and then to place you in a setting where you can be yourself in service to Him.

Out of this freedom come hearts full of praise, worship, and joy. Out of this freedom come bodies willing to serve as living sacrifices. Out of this freedom come gifts that are described in Romans chapters 8 and 12. Paul explains the outworking, the overflow, and the freedom that come from Christ's greatest gift—the gift of salvation. This purchase was not made by anything that you or I did or ever can do.

The following diagram outlines the legal case that will unfold in the book of Romans:

ROMANS: MANKIND VS. GOD						
EVENTS						
Introduction	Prosecution's Evidence	Defense's Cross Examination	Defense's Evidence	Judge's Sovereignty	Freedom	Farewell
CHAPTERS						
1:1-17	1.18-3.20	3.21-26	4-8	9-11	12-15	16

The revelation that comes from the book of Romans is able to free you from all bondages, or anything else that would hold you back. It frees you from unnatural relations, from the worship of created things, from cursing and bitterness, and all of the other sins addressed in the Romans book and elsewhere. It frees you into increasing measures of faith, hope, and love. You are free by the Judge's decree!

There are at least three basic ways of studying the book of Romans: a simple outline approach (see Appendix 2), a tree metaphor outline (see Appendix 3), and a courtroom metaphor. In this book I will major in the courtroom metaphor where our salvation was legally declared.

Chapter 1
A LEGAL TRANSACTION

Imagine yourself as the accused sitting in a courtroom. God the Father sits as Judge during your criminal trial and you are silenced in His presence. His judgment alone will determine your guilt or innocence. You feel the stare of the devilish prosecutor and the tension of the ghastly spectators with a sense of impending doom in your heart. You sense the weight of the incriminating evidence about to be revealed. At the same time, you are grateful when Jesus Christ stands by your side serving as your Defense Attorney. Relief and despair collide when you notice that you are not the only defendant in this heavenly court. Every sinner that ever lived, whether good, gross, or religious, stands with you at the judgment. This scenario is the Romans story. Jesus Christ served as your Defense Himself when He secured your eternal freedom by taking your verdict upon Himself. God the Father formulated this surprisingly judicious plan before the foundation of the world. He then carefully orchestrated the plan, disclosing it first through the Old Testament prophets and later to the New Testament apostles.

UNDERSTANDING THE BOOK OF ROMANS IS ABSOLUTELY NECESSARY IN ORDER TO BUILD A STRONG, RIGHTEOUS FOUNDATION FOR OUR LIVES.

Understanding the book of Romans is absolutely necessary in order to build a strong, righteous foundation for our lives. We see, in an overview of the book, our flawed natures, the state in which

God found us, and the way in which He makes us right. We will learn why we need to be right in His eyes, how we get right, and what it will do for us once we are. Romans reveals to us our human condemnation, complete justification (to defend with reason), continuous sanctification (to free from sin), divine vindication (to clear from accusation), and practical consecration (to devote to a purpose).

In order for the revelation of Romans to be complete, we must begin with a revelation of who we were, before we can have a full revelation of who we shall be. Picture your life inside a skyscraper. Some of us think we started out on the fourth floor of an upper-crust department store when we really started out as cellar dwellers in a condemned building. We entered the elevator, pushed the button, and rose to the seventh floor. We thought we only had to rise three floors when, in actuality, we had to rise seven floors and move on to another place just to get where we would like to be. We began down in a stinking, rotten, filthy, moldy, creepy, and slimy basement. There were fearful animals and deadly viruses surrounding us. We hoped to end on the rooftop of a brand new edifice, looking out over a whole city amid the blazing sun. We will not fully appreciate the view and the blazing sun atop any new place until we understand the spiritually slimy, creepy, mucky, sloppy place from which we came. Many of us do not fully understand the depths from which we came; thus, we do not fully comprehend or appreciate what Jesus Christ has done for us.

Romans' author, the apostle Paul, wants to make sure that the revelation of our depravity (corruption) is exposed in the full, noonday sun. By the time the revelation is full and the sun is blazing in the sky, our eyes are achy because, somehow, we cannot handle that much light. What Jesus Christ has legally done for us is glorious. This is a fact, not an emotion. Emotions follow facts, and our salvation is a factual legal transaction.

The book of Romans is a book about that legal transaction. It is written as a document that would appeal to a lawyer. In fact, when people studied law years ago, the book of Romans was one of the texts they had to study in order to find out how the apostle Paul made a case. Those law students thought it was the apostle who made the compelling argument, but it was really the Holy Spirit making the case through Paul for our justification. God really is on our side! Truly, Romans is a brilliant document in any court of law!

TRULY, ROMANS IS A BRILLIANT DOCUMENT IN ANY COURT OF LAW!

Chapter 2
KEY TO ROMANS: RIGHTEOUSNESS

As the case proceeds, one word stands out through repetition prior to Paul's presentation of the prosecution's condemning evidence. That one word is "Gospel," meaning "good news." Before Paul presents the heavy bad news, he declares the weightier good news: "For I am not ashamed of the Gospel (good news) *of Christ*" (Rom. 1.16a). Once you realize the book of Romans reveals what this Gospel really means, you will want to preach, publish, and sing about it with fresh appreciation.

THE GOSPEL

What is this "Gospel (good news) of *and* from God" (Rom. 1.1b)? According to Romans 1:16 *(KJV)* and 15:16 *(KJV),* the Gospel of Christ is "the power of God unto salvation to every one that believeth" and "the gospel of God." This good news comes from God Himself.

To see the depth and width of this Gospel, one needs to look at some of the other Scriptures where "Gospel" is referenced. The Gospel is "the gospel of his Son" (*KJV*, Rom. 1.9), and "the gospel of your salvation" (*KJV*, Eph. 1.13). The Gospel is "the gospel of the grace of God" (*KJV*, Acts 20.24) and "the Gospel of peace" (Eph. 6.15). The word "Gospel" is linked to God's Son, your salvation, God's grace, and peace. It is also the "gospel of the kingdom" (*KJV*, Matt. 24.14), it is the "good news of a great joy which will come to all the people" (Lk. 2.10), and it is "God's power working unto salvation (for the deliverance from eternal death) to everyone who believes" (Rom. 1.16). The apostle quotes Isaiah when he says, "How beautiful are the feet of them that preach the gospel of peace, and bring glad tidings of good things!" (*KJV*, Rom. 10.15).

When my wife and I were living on a mission station, six-hundred miles from the coast of Kenya, I was reminded of these verses as I looked up to see four men approaching the mission, carrying a very heavy bed weighing much more than the skeleton of a man on it. He was barely alive. His friends had carried him, taking turns with four other friends, to this place where he could get help. As the men placed the heavy bed down at the edge of the mission, they said, "Missionary, help our friend. We have carried him many miles." Immediately, we took him to the nearest clinic. I was extremely grateful that my wife and I had brought the Good News of the Gospel to a people who had been sitting in darkness but now found a place of healing.

GOD POWER OR WILL POWER?

In the universe, there are many kinds of power. The Bible refers in the book of Esther to the power in the nations (1.3), in Job as the power of the sword (5.20), in Proverbs as the power of speech (18.21), in Daniel as the power of animals (6.27), in Romans as the power of the spirit world (8.38), in Titus as the power of government (3.1), and in Luke as Satan's power (10.19).

Everyone puts his or her faith in some kind of power. Although people have faith, not many think about what they put their faith in. It is good to ask oneself, "What exactly do I have faith in?" The apostle Paul answers the question for us who believe with "God's power" (Rom. 1.16). Your faith can be no stronger than the thing or person in which you believe. Believers in Jesus Christ wholeheartedly place their faith in God's tremendous, surpassing power, which is able to turn a sinner into a saint.

Have you ever experienced a time when you were failing, and it looked as though you were down for the count? This was a time when Satan stood over you declaring, "You're out!" and he further intimidated by pointing out all of the spectators throwing towels at you and shouting, "Give up!" What is it that has the power to put you back on your feet at a time like this? Is it your will or is it God's power? Is it saying, "I'll grit my teeth and get up again. I have the will power!"? You may choose to have faith in your will and credit human will power for an apparent victory. Or, is it God who has the power to lift you up when your will is weak and you feel defeated? You must choose to put your faith in His tremendous resurrection power to lift you to new life. Your will power may be good for some limited things, but to become righteous requires the power and Spirit of God.

YOUR FAITH CAN BE NO STRONGER THAN THE THING OR PERSON IN WHICH YOU BELIEVE.

God wants to give us His tremendous power—the power of salvation! God's power is for everyone who trusts in Christ. Salvation is available to all who believe. Romans 1.16 emphatically states, "For I am not ashamed of the Gospel (good news) of Christ; for it is God's power working unto salvation (for deliverance from eternal death) to every one who believes with a personal trust and a confident surrender and firm reliance, to the Jew first and also to the Greek."

I once heard a relevant testimony about a missionary working with a tribe to translate the Bible into a tribal language. Translating a language is made easier when a person can point to a concrete object and the native word for the object is spoken. However, it is more difficult to translate concepts like "to believe." While this missionary was pondering how to translate "to believe," he traveled with some native porters of the tribe to another village. In order to get there they had to cross a vine bridge over a large ravine. The natives strode boldly out onto the bridge, but when the missionary approached the vine bridge, he refused to cross. He did not trust the bridge even when the natives assured him, "Put all of your weight on the bridge and it will hold you." To this day, "to believe" in this tribe's translation of Acts 16.31 reads something like "put all of your weight on Jesus and you will be saved."

RIGHTEOUSNESS NOT OUR OWN

The word "righteousness" is used frequently to focus on the main issue in this case. "For in the Gospel a righteousness which God ascribes is revealed" (Rom. 1.17a). Verses 16 and 17 are the key verses and thrust of the book of Romans. What is the Gospel all about? It is a revelation of righteousness that God ascribes or demands. In this Gospel righteousness is revealed, both springing from faith and leading to faith. The key word is righteousness.

If you truly understand God's righteousness, you must admit that everything you ever did or will do to earn your salvation is entirely as filthy rags (Isa. 64.6). Only in the Gospel is God's righteousness provided. *Righteousness* is a beautiful word meaning "right standing" with God. It includes being made conformable to Him. Righteousness is *rightness.* I was wrong; now I stand in His *rightness.*

How many us have to be right all of the time? If someone says you are wrong, you are offended. You might continue on by trying to defend your own *rightness.* The apostle Paul wrote in Philippians 3.9: ". . . not having any (self-achieved) righteousness that can be called my own . . ." What a liberating truth this is! You and I do not have to be right all of the time because our true righteousness (*rightness*) in Christ is assured.

We cannot accept full salvation until we accept the fact that we are totally wrong because God's righteousness is revealed from heaven alone. This righteousness, according to Romans 1.17 is ". . . both springing from faith and leading to faith—disclosed through the way of faith which arouses to more faith. As it is written, The man who through faith is just *and* upright shall live *and* shall live by faith."

IT'S TIME TO ENTER THE COURTROOM.

PART II

COURTROOM: PROSECUTION'S EVIDENCE

Chapter 3
PRESENT IN THE COURTROOM: SERVANT, SAVIOR, SAINTS & SINNERS

Imagine yourself in a heavenly courtroom. The court is brought to order. The major courtroom characters are introduced in chapter 1 of Romans. The first two individuals introduced are the servant and the Savior. The servant Paul will accurately report the events in the case of *God vs. Mankind.* He introduces himself first and then Jesus Christ, the Savior of mankind, whose perfect justice can vindicate each guilty defendant. Finally, two groups of courtroom defendants, the saints and the sinners, are introduced.

SERVANT

Paul, the witness to the trial, starts by painting a fourteen-point "self-portrait" of himself in Romans 1. What exactly does he say about himself?

First, he introduces himself as "Paul, *a servant of Jesus Christ*" (emphasis added, *KJV*, Rom. 1.1a). The Amplified translation of Romans 1.1 states, "From Paul, a bond servant of Jesus Christ, the Messiah, called to be an apostle, a (special messenger) set apart to [preach] the Gospel (good news) of and from God." In the original Greek, the word for servant Paul uses here is *doulos*, meaning "a servant, a slave, or a bond servant." A servant's or a slave's identity is based on whomever he or she serves.

If someone were to ask you, "Well, what are you?" and you reply, "I am a servant," a negative connotation may come to mind. But, if you were to answer, "I am a servant of the good King," your work would take on an entirely different meaning because you take your identity from the one you serve. A common problem faced by many pastors and Christian workers is they mistakenly serve people and feel they are getting the short end of the stick every time. They do their best and no one seems to appreciate it.

The apostle Paul did not make the mistake of serving people first. He confessed he is first *a servant of Jesus Christ.* When you confess that you are a servant of Jesus Christ, it gives your life an unshakable identity. Jesus keeps giving abundant life to the measure of the responsibility He has assigned you. As His servant you serve Him by serving others.

Paul does not stop at confessing he is first of all a servant of Jesus Christ; he continues on to say that he is *"called to be an apostle"* (emphasis added, 1a). An apostle is one who has been arrested by God, who has been chosen and appointed, or who has been sent out possibly as a missionary or an ambassador establishing churches and pastors. Paul was a servant by personal devotion; he was an apostle by divine election. All people who offer themselves to God as servants will come to know His divine election or calling. You cannot say, "I will be an apostle." You may, however, say, "I will be a servant." The calling and election of God must be the calling and election of *God;* it does not originate with men (see 1 Cor. 12.11 and Rom. 11.29). God is the one who called and separated him to be an apostle. True apostles are never self-appointed.

PAUL WAS A SERVANT BY PERSONAL DEVOTION; HE WAS AN APOSTLE BY DIVINE ELECTION.

What exactly is our part? We need to offer ourselves as servants. In Old Testament times a love slave made a decision to serve a master, "Then his master shall bring him unto the judges; he shall also bring him to the door, or unto the door post; and his master shall bore his ear through with an awl; and he shall serve him for ever" (*KJV*, Ex. 21.6). In other words, there was no release from this love relationship commitment. Someone may be tempted to say, "I'm tired of serving God. I'm going to quit. I've had enough." This person may have been serving only people and forgot his or her service is to a loving heavenly Father God. When a servant of the loving God offers a cup of cold water in His name, He says that act will be honored because it was done in His name (see Matt. 10.42). In everything you do, you are to serve a loving God who ministers through you to the needs of mankind. Your reward comes from Him!

Paul describes himself further in verse 1 as "*separated unto the gospel*" (emphasis added, *KJV*). He has been set apart and sanctified for this ministry. The same word for "separated" here he uses in Galatians 1.15 to mean "separated from my mother's womb." That means from the moment he was conceived, God appointed him to a unique and holy calling.

Acts 13.2b records, "Separate now for Me Barnabas and Saul for the work for which I have called them." Here to separate means to designate, to mark out by fixed limits, to bind as a field, or to set apart from someone else. If you own a hundred acre field, you could mark off a little section to plant strawberries. You designate it for a special purpose. Each one of us has been marked for a special purpose. We have each been set apart by God from the rest of the field. He plants us in certain places and puts boundaries around our lives.

Paul declares his calling in verse 5 (*KJV*), "By whom we have received grace and apostleship . . ." Now he says that he is a *recipient of* two things: *grace and apostleship.* From heaven come His grace for salvation and divine selection for service. Both come from the hand of God. Paul, the writer and witness to a "heavenly court case," says that he has received grace to be saved and has received apostleship for ministry. For this he has offered himself as a lifelong love slave to his good Master.

"First, I thank my God through Jesus Christ for all of you" (8a). Paul describes himself as *a giver of thanks.* In Romans 1.21 we will learn that one of the world's first downward steps is a lack of thankfulness, but here Paul stresses that he himself is thankful "for all of you" (8a). Giving thanks for everyone opens up the door of divine blessing through you to the people you serve. You can never bless a people for whom you have not given thanks. When you criticize and find fault, they will return you the favor. There is no blessing happening. Agree with Paul, "First, I thank my God through Jesus Christ for all of you." As a leader, the Spirit has reminded me to pray earnestly for all those I lead. In fact, the command to me personally was, "If you do not plead you cannot lead."

In verse 9 Paul explains, "For God is my witness, Whom I serve with [all] my spirit . . . ." Paul is *sincere.* The word "serve" here indicates a service of worship basic to all true Christian service. Paul wants his audience to be assured that he sincerely serves with his whole heart in the Gospel.

Paul continues to paint his self-portrait in verse 9 (*KJV*): ". . . that without ceasing I make mention of you always in my prayers . . ." Paul had a *prayer life,* not simply a prayer time. People who only have a prayer time may think, "I have had my fifteen minutes of prayer this morning, and I have fulfilled my obligation." What about the rest of the day? Paul *prayed without ceasing* for all the saints, not just himself.

Paul describes himself as a very *submitted* person in verse 10: "I keep pleading that somehow by God's will I may now at last be prospered and come to you." A person submitted to God will always submit *"by God's will"* (emphasis added) to proposed plans. It was not God's will for Paul to travel to Rome when Paul originally planned, so he waited. When we plan our lives *"by God's will"* (emphasis added), we must watch for His red lights as well as His green lights.

What may be learned about Paul from verse 11? He had *a desire to impart something spiritual* to others. "For I am yearning to see you, that I may impart and share with you some spiritual gift to strengthen and establish you." Whatever you minister from is what you minister to. If you minister from your head, you minister to people's heads. If you minister from your heart, you minister to their hearts. If you minister from your life, you minister to their lives. When you minister by the Spirit, you minister to their spirits.

WHATEVER YOU MINISTER FROM IS WHAT YOU MINISTER TO.

Paul's greatest desire was to see the church in Rome in person in order to impart something spiritual to them. Could it be that our motive in going to see people is to get a gift or a word from the Lord? Paul desired to go to give. If you go to impart, you will receive His reward. Is your ministry one of information or of formation? God is calling us to a ministry of impartation—to impart into people's lives—to impart life, faith, and love to those who are in need. You can only impart life by the Holy Spirit of God when people are ready to receive. Only true Spirit and Word impartation will produce Divine inspiration.

Verse 12 states, "That is, that we may be mutually strengthened and encouraged and comforted by each other's faith, both yours and mine." Paul needs others and they need him. He did not isolate himself from the whole Body of Christ. Paul fully expects when he does get to Rome, the blessing will be in mutual giving and receiving. His *desire to share and receive* of the blessings of the Lord will be fulfilled.

Paul uncovers more of himself in verse 13a, "I want you to know, brethren, that many times I have planned and intended to come to you." He is *eager*. Have you ever met Christians who sit around and say, "God knows where I am when He wants me"? Paul did not wastefully sit around; he actively prayed and planned while he "waited." In prayer God is able to alert you to a need. "By God's will" He will make clear His divine purpose for you. Maybe His plan for you is for a specific city, an inner city, or even another country. Start to investigate like Moses at the burning bush until you receive instructions. Remember Paul's words, ". . . many times I have planned and intended to come to you."

In verse 14 (*KJV*) Paul confesses, ". . . I am *debtor* . . ." (emphasis added). What Paul said about himself, we may freely say about ourselves. Since you and I have received so much from God, we have a love obligation to all people who have not yet heard the "good news." We are debtors to love.

Paul assures his readers in verse 15a (*KJV*), "So, as much as in me is, I am ready to preach the gospel." Paul felt the weight of the love debt he owed others and was *prepared and ready always to preach.* You could go to church on a Sunday morning when someone unexpectedly asks you to teach a class. "Who? Me, a substitute teacher?" you may annoyingly think. When you are always prepared you are fully able to share out of the riches of God's Word and to do an exceedingly excellent substitute job. Are you able to say with Paul, "I am prepared and ready"?

"For I am *not ashamed* of the Gospel (good news) of Christ" Paul confesses in verse 16a (emphasis added). Despite the fact Paul had many earthly achievements of which he could boast, the only thing for which he did boast was the Gospel of Christ. He does not boast about himself, but about the gift of salvation he has received. He is *not ashamed* of the Gospel.

SAVIOR

As Paul introduces himself in chapter 1 of Romans, he simultaneously weaves in a résumé of the Defense Attorney Jesus Christ. Jesus is the sinners' Savior Who is central throughout Romans. Paul reports the following seven qualifications of this heaven-sent Savior—our Lawyer:

- In verse 3 (*KJV*) he describes the ultimate *distinctive character* of this Savior, "Concerning his Son Jesus Christ our Lord . . ." The Savior is *the one and only perfect Son of God.*

- In verse 3 Paul refers to Jesus Christ as not only the Son of God, but also as "to the flesh (His human nature) . . . descended from David." He is a descendant of King David. His *human identity* may be historically traced.

- He is both the heavenly Son of God and the human Son of man. He is *uniquely both fully God and fully man.* Jesus Christ has a *unique identity* that makes Him solely qualified to be our Savior.

- When Paul calls Jesus Christ "our Lord" in verse 4, he attributes *supreme authority* over mankind to Jesus Christ. He does not say that Jesus is one of many lords. He names Jesus alone as "our Lord." As our Lord, Jesus has supreme authority, and is the only trustworthy One.

- Jesus Christ's *victorious triumphant act* was *His own resurrection from the dead.* Verse 4b states, He "was openly designated the Son of God in power—in a striking, triumphant and miraculous manner—by His resurrection from the dead, even Jesus Christ our Lord." The greatest historical fact in all of eternity is the *resurrection of Jesus Christ from the dead.* Discoveries in science, math, and medicine, etc., are great, but the greatest disclosure in all of time is the triumphant act of the resurrection of Jesus Christ from the dead!

- He brings with His unique position an *established position of great power.*

- He ". . . was openly designated the Son of God in power . . ." (4). His *established position* is one *of great power and authority.*

- Jesus Christ has a *moral right to power,* for He rules "according to the Spirit of holiness" (4a). All of His actions are virtuous because He and the Spirit of holiness are One. When we move with the Spirit of holiness, we too rule in holiness. The vessels must be holy if they are to be used of God. (Lev. 20.26)

THE VESSELS MUST BE HOLY
IF THEY ARE TO BE USED OF GOD.

SAINTS

Paul includes in chapter 1 an account of the blessings for the courtroom saints. He keeps the victorious end in mind as he begins with the exciting account of sinners turned to saints.

Saints are called. "And this includes yourselves, called of Jesus Christ *and* invited [as you are] to belong to Him" (6). The *saints* are *the called ones* who are called by an outward solicitation of preaching, and a simultaneous response to the inward drawing of the Holy Spirit. What are the saints called to? Saints are called to "belong to Him" in a "consecrated life" (7).

Saints are loved. What a position to be in as ". . . all God's beloved ones . . ." (7). God's entire wrath is taken away from His loved ones. Saints are beloved by God, period. They are saints in process, called "to be" (see verse 7) saints. They are justified beloved ones as they are becoming sanctified and perfected.

Saints are recipients. Right after Paul addresses the beloved saints in verse 7, he proclaims a blessing on them, "Grace and spiritual blessing and peace be yours from God our Father and from the Lord Jesus Christ." Saints are receivers of His grace, His forgiveness, blessing, and peace.

SINNERS

The final group of courtroom characters introduced by Paul are the sinners (see Rom. 1.18-32). The apostle primarily addresses the book to the saints in Rome; however, he does not fail to make it clear we are all sinners without God. There are three types of sinners Paul describes—"gross" sinners, "good" sinners, and "religious" sinners. The whole human race is made up of sinners. Each type of sinner will be explained further in chapters 5, 6 and 7 of this book.

Chapter 4
HOW BAD IS THE EVIDENCE?

For God's (holy) wrath and indignation are revealed from heaven against all ungodliness and unrighteousness of men, who in their wickedness repress *and* hinder the truth *and* make it inoperative" (Rom. 1.18). How bad is the evidence against the human race? The hungry prosecutor respectfully addresses the Judge as **"Your Honor"** as the entire human race stands before the bench to hear the evidence.

Paul begins his opening remarks with the hard evidence being presented in the courtroom against the defendants:

> For God's (holy) wrath and indignation are revealed from heaven against all ungodliness and unrighteousness of men, who in their wickedness repress and hinder the truth and make it inoperative. For that which is known about God is evident to them and made plain in their inner consciousness, because God (Himself) has shown it to them. For ever since the creation of the world His invisible nature and attributes, that is, His eternal power and divinity have been made intelligible and clearly discernible in and through the things that have been made—His handiworks. So (men) are without excuse—altogether without any defense or justification. (Rom. 1.18-20)

"Your Honor," continues the prosecutor, "mankind is without excuse, altogether without any defense or justification. Even if a person has never heard Your Gospel, there is no excuse because You have provided the picture book of creation that clearly speaks of the Creator. The whole world is wholly guilty."

"Wholly guilty?" questions the Judge. "That is a very strong statement you are making."

"Yes," accuses the prosecution. "When you hear the rest of the case, You will agree that this mankind You created is entirely guilty with no excuse!"

After hearing the first of the accusations, the defendants try to defend themselves by saying things like, "Hey, I am not like that. I don't hide the truth, and I love God." On and on some of us go naming things we did and did not do. We may not see ourselves in the evidence presented thus far; however, there is more to come. You will be included; none will escape.

RIGHTEOUSNESS AND WRATH

We know from Romans 1.17 that righteousness from God is revealed from heaven. Then in verse 18 we learn that wrath also is revealed from heaven: "For God's [holy] wrath and indignation are revealed from heaven . . ." Some people mistakenly think that righteousness is revealed from heaven and wrath is revealed from hell. No. God is the source of both. God's wrath is revealed from heaven against all ungodliness and unrighteousness. God's righteousness is offered to whoever will receive it.

Ungodliness or *un-God-likeness* manifests itself in idolatry. This means man makes other gods besides the one true God. Idolatry is manifested when you or I expect to receive from things or people that which only comes from God. There are certain intangibles like true happiness, joy, and contentment that are only God-given. When I expect that a new house, new spouse, new car, or new anything will bring me something that only God can deliver, then that thing becomes an idol. For example, some married person might say,

"I'm just not happy in this marriage, and I deserve to be happy." This kind of discontented person is unfulfilled because he or she looks at marriage as the source of happiness. "If another partner can be found, then true happiness will surely be achieved," the discontented one mistakenly thinks. True joy and real happiness come from God alone. There is no substitute. God's wrath is revealed against all forms of idolatry.

God's wrath is also revealed against unrighteousness. While ungodliness is sin against God, unrighteousness is sin against fellow human beings. The first is on a vertical level; the latter is horizontal. *Ungodly* and *unrighteous* describe the character of those who are under the wrath of God. This unrighteousness is not because people are ignorant of the truth. They know better, yet they "repress and hinder the truth and make it inoperative" (18b). Unrighteous people are not ignorant people. Unrighteous people are those who have heard the Gospel, but who choose not to believe it. We are all unrighteous before we come to know Jesus Christ. Heaven's wrath is sent not as the judgment for ignorance, but the penalty for rejection of truth. People know the truth and choose to reject it.

Meanwhile, in the courtroom, the prosecution's evidence is mounting.

ALL ARE WITHOUT EXCUSE

"Your Honor," the prosecutor boasts, "I will prove that every last one of these defendants is without excuse, based on four basic facts. The first fact is that *God can be known.* Wherever anyone travels in this world, people know there is a God—a Creator. Occasionally some 'enlightened' people try to prove there is no God. All nations know there is a spirit world. Some people are convinced that if they don't see it, it does not exist. In fact, Your Word claims the opposite—even though they do not see it, they know that the unseen world exists."

"The second fact is that *man has the capacity to know God.* Mankind manifests the capacity to know You, **Your Honor,"** the prosecutor reasons. "This means man has the ability to know there is a God even if he has never heard the Gospel."

The accuser approaches the bench, turns, and points toward the nervous defendants as he continues, "Therefore, these slimy defendants cannot sincerely ask the questions 'Are the heathen really lost?' or 'How can God judge that person?' There is no room for their lame excuses because these sinners were provided plenty of opportunity to know You exist."

"Furthermore," he adds, "*God has specifically revealed Himself in creation* to you sinners, even to those who never heard the Gospel. Psalm 19.1-4 in the *King James Version* of the Bible says, 'The heavens declare the glory of God; and the firmament showeth his handiwork. Day unto day uttereth speech, and night unto night showeth knowledge. There is no speech nor language, where their voice is not heard. Their line is gone out through all the earth, and their words to the end of the world . . .' The earth is God's object lesson. The Old Testament contains more than adequate proof that God has revealed Himself through creation. Psalm 8.3, 19.4, 143.5, Isaiah 42.5, 45.18 and Job 12.7-9 provide additional proof that God is revealed in creation."

As soon as Paul hears the prosecution's third point he thinks to himself, "Someone may still doubtfully argue, 'You mean, people can know how to be saved without ever hearing the Gospel?' However, the Bible does not say that people can be saved through creation's revelation; it only says that people are able to understand certain aspects of God by observing creation. It says that creation points to a Creator."

"I am not finished," the complainant continues; "The fourth fact is related to the third in that *mankind is able to know three specific characteristics about God Himself from creation.* These defendants know His *invisible nature,* His *eternal power,* and His *divinity.*"

Paul is amazed at the prosecutor's ability to use truth to accuse his feeble foes. Specific things about God may be known without a written word, but Paul desires to leave God's beloved with hard evidence himself, so he pens Romans 1.19-20: "For that which is known about God is evident to them and made plain in their inner consciousness, because God [Himself] has shown it to them. For ever since the creation of the world His invisible nature and attributes, that is, His eternal power and divinity have been made intelligible and clearly discernible in and through the things that have been made—His handiworks. So [men] are without excuse—altogether without any defense or justification."

The first characteristic made understandable to all is *"His invisible nature."* Moffatt's translation states, "For ever since the world was created, his invisible nature" (Rom. 1.20a). The first thing anyone can know about God is that He is invisible. Does a person need to read a Bible to find that out? No, anyone can perceive that the One who made earth and heaven, hills, mountains, and rivers is invisible, and can be knowable.

The second knowable detail is *"His eternal power."* This means He exists from everlasting to everlasting. People who know God only through creation can know He is limitless as they observe the distant stars and infinite space. His power is everlasting.

The third characteristic made known to all is His *"divinity."* All peoples and tribes are conscious of a spiritual supreme being. Many offer sacrifices to unknown deities because they accept this as a fact. Many "sense" a "supernatural" presence in their daily lives.

Are the heathen, then, really a lost case? Yes. They are utterly lost. Why? How can God be love and declare men lost? He is able to do so based on these four truths: God can be known, man has the capacity to know God, God has revealed Himself in creation, and creation reveals God's invisible nature, His eternal power, and His divinity. If people who have never heard the Gospel accept the revelation of God as spoken in creation, the eternal God will continue to reveal Himself to them. He wants to reveal Himself to man in the person of His Son, Jesus Christ. However, some people choose to worship idols rather than "the invisible God."

THE HUMAN RACE IS WITHOUT EXCUSE

It is in this divine courtroom that you and I will be found guilty or declared free. The pronouncement will not be a feeling or a passing blessing. It will be a legally binding declaration. Justice will be served. We are in the Supreme Court of the universe where the final Judge of all mankind presides!

The defendants boast, "We can fight our own battles. We will represent ourselves" while they conspire to think of a way to deny or hide the prosecution's facts. None seemed to have noticed the sign outside above the courtroom door stating the old adage: "He who defends himself defends a fool."

Chapter 5

THE "GROSS" SINNER

The Judge calls the court to order. "Quiet in this courtroom!" He directs. "You defendants will have your turn to defend yourselves. But, for now, is the prosecution prepared to present further evidence?"

"Yes, **Your Honor.** In fact, by their own conceits, I have divided the whole lot of them into three categories of sinners: 'gross' sinners, 'good' sinners, and 'religious' sinners. While You and I agree that all three types were born sinners, they have all progressed to further degeneration over time."

THE PROCESS OF DEGENERATION

Verses 21-23

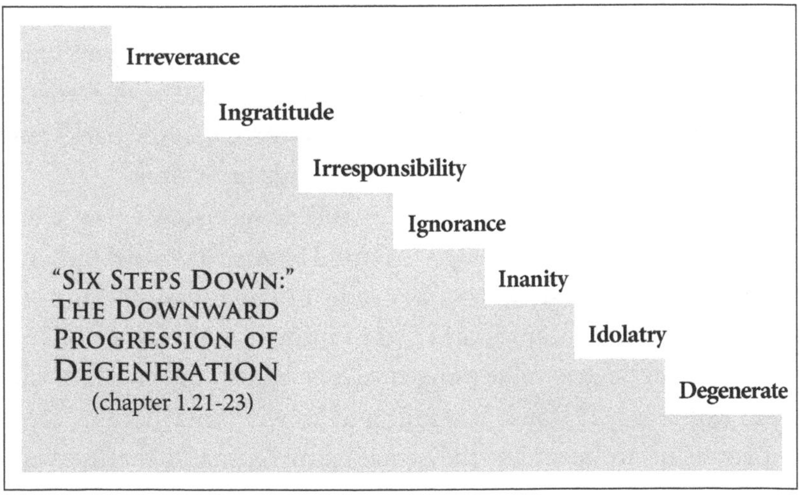

The first downward step of degeneration is *Irreverence.* Romans 1.21 (*KJV*) states, "Because that, when they know God, they glorified him not as God. This downward trend starts when humans know God but do not want to glorify God. J.B. Phillips' translation of the Bible says, "They knew Him all the time as a God" (Rom. 1.21a). People the world over accept there is a God; however, sometimes a misleading education or deceiving philosophy puts doubt in their hearts. They know all the time there is a God, yet they refuse to acknowledge Him as such.

The second downward spiral is *Ingratitude*: ". . . neither were thankful (21). When you do not worship God for who He is, you are not thankful for what He does. This same ungrateful spirit can infect Christians whenever they do not worship Him for who He is.

Irresponsibility is the third degenerative downward movement. Rather than taking on personal responsibility, these people become vain in their imaginations and blame others. Berkeley's translation says it this way, "They indulged in their speculations (21).

WHEN YOU DO NOT WORSHIP GOD FOR WHO HE IS, YOU ARE NOT THANKFUL FOR WHAT HE DOES.

Fourthly, degenerate sinners coil downward to *Ignorance.* Romans 1.21 (*NIV*) states, ". . . their foolish hearts were darkened." Berkeley elaborates, "Their stupid minds were all in the dark" and Moffatt confirms, "Till their ignorant minds grew dark."

The prosecuting attorney takes full advantage of this statement by reminding the Judge, **"Your Honor,** these defendants' foolish hearts were darkened. Instead of being open and honest, these defendants became darkened in mind and thought."

The fifth degenerative move down is *Inanity* or senseless silliness. Romans 1.22 states, "Claiming to be wise, they became fools —professing to be smart, they made simpletons of themselves." J.B. Phillips puts it, "Behind a façade of 'wisdom,' they became just fools. Finally, the *New English Bible* translates this verse, "They boast of their wisdom, but they have made fools of themselves.

The world's culture continually tries to deceive and influence us using "*The Emperor's New Clothes* syndrome." The world says, "Oh, yes, Your Highness, you really have on some beautiful clothes!" Then some little child comes along and says, "Looks like you are naked to me." A worldly person rebukes, "You are so ignorant. You have to be 'enlightened' to see these clothes." The innocent child is made to look "stupid" because the child does not see the invisible clothes that the world "sees." Who is really foolish? Who is really honest?

The final downward movement is the step to *Idolatry*. The latter half of verse 23 says, the glory of God was "exchanged for and represented by images, resembling mortal man and birds and beasts and reptiles." Even their idols degenerate into worshipping images of mortal man, birds, beasts and reptiles.

THE PRODUCT OF DEGENERATION

Verses 24-32

Romans, chapter 1, uncovers the deadly consequences to this process of degeneration. The first result is mentioned in verse 24, where it states, "God gave them up." The second is in verse 26, "God gave them up." The third is located in verse 28, "God gave them over" (*KJV*).

Whom is God giving up or over? God is handing over the "gross" sinners to their own ways. The product of their "badness" is that God ". . . gave them up . . . to sexual impurity, to the dishonoring of their bodies among themselves, abandoning them to the degrading power of sin" (24). It is truly amazing how mankind quickly moves into sexual impurity as a consequence of turning away from a Holy God.

God gives them up to their foul desires. The J.B. Phillips translation puts it this way: "God gave them up—to be the playthings of their own foul desires in dishonouring their own bodies." This does not leave much room for the imagination. The *New English Bible* states, "God has given them up to the vileness of their own desires, and the consequent degradation of their bodies . . . ." Moffatt's translation echoes, "So God has given them up, in their hearts' lust, to sexual vice, the dishonouring of their own bodies . . ." Father God spells out the consequences of the degeneration process very clearly, "If you want to do your own thing, I am taking my hands off. Have it your way. I love you, but I cannot condone your unrighteous conduct." Thus, these people choose to become playthings for each other's foul unmentionable desires.

Why does God the Father give them up? Part of the answer lies in verse 25, "Because they exchanged the truth of God for a lie and worshipped and served the creature rather than the Creator, Who is blessed forever! Amen—so be it." He gives them up because they bartered away the true, living God for a false god. All sinners have left the One who created them. They have rejected the Word and the Spirit, leaving no avenue for conviction. Life becomes foolish and aimless without God at the center.

Remember, certain things may be known of God. Instead of worshipping the Creator God, degenerative people worship His creation. As a result, they exchange the true God for false images, which they worship. "These men deliberately forfeited the truth of God and accepted a lie, paying homage and giving service to the creature instead of to the Creator, who alone is worthy to be worshipped for ever and ever, amen" (*Phillips,* 25).

"Your Honor, these 'gross' sinners reject divine worship in favor of creature worship."

Does creature worship sound familiar in our current world culture? Recently, at an airport in Europe I saw "sex shops" in the waiting lounge. People who are self-deluded from "enlightened" education have drifted without the anchor of truth. In their thinking the truth is suppressed, held down, and hindered. How great is this darkness!

Do your peers think the Bible is an old-fashioned book? If

someone you know thinks the Bible is a book for the Victorian or Puritan Age and only applies to people like Moses or Jesus, then introduce them to Romans. You could begin reading in chapter 1 at about verse 20. When your peers hear the Bible speak about present day gross behavior in such graphic terms, there can be no argument that the Bible is not relevant for today. People who have embraced the present culture and are not familiar with the Bible draw incorrect conclusions about God's standards. They will be surprised that Romans chapter 1 leaves nothing to the imagination.

The second mention of God's "giving them up" is in verse 26. Paul mentions God is giving them up to "disgraceful passions" (*Phillips*) and "shameful passions" (*New English Bible*). The word here for "passions" really means "perverted passions." This is not simply a man and a woman misdirected in their love for each other. These are people (possibly of the same sex) in lustful, perverted actions. "Aberrations" is another meaning of the word "passions." This is not love; this is lust. The things these people are doing are completely indecent, things about which we are embarrassed to talk. Why is the world very forward on this subject? They refer to it as "coming out of the closet." These indecent actions are portrayed as right on television and other media. The world is blatant because they have bartered God away. "And the men also turned from natural relations with women and were set ablaze (burned out, consumed) with lust for one another" (27).

Meanwhile, in the courtroom, the prosecutor boldly proclaims, **"Your Honor,** I call your attention to these sinners who are so gross even their rightful, natural, healthy use of sex intended by God is no longer being fulfilled. They suffer in their own bodies and personalities the inevitable consequences and penalty of their going astray, which is a fitting start to their retribution."

The leaven of degradation continues to permeate human history, and I am amazed at the number of people, even those who have claimed to be Christians, who now accept that homosexuality is an alternate lifestyle. Even homosexual priests and ministers are being ordained. When you and I do not agree with this practice, we may be accused of being too "narrow-minded," "ignorant," or "behind-the-times." If by narrow-minded any accusers mean that we who disapprove of homosexuality hold to the "narrow way" of God's truth, then we should remain narrowly focused, for the broad way leads to destruction (Matt. 7.13).

Paul's third reference to the degradation process is located in verse 28, "And so, since they did not see fit to acknowledge God or approve of Him or consider Him worth the knowing, God gave them over to a base and condemned mind to do things not proper or decent but loathsome." He not only gives them over to foul desires and to perverted passions, but Phillips says, ". . . He allowed them to become the slaves of their degenerate minds." The *New English Bible* states, ". . . He has given them up to their own depraved reason." Mankind wallows in the filth of unrighteousness when he turns from God's offer of purity and godliness. When there is no "god-like-ness," there is "un-right-ness." The reason God gives people over to a reprobate mind is that they refuse to retain God in their knowledge and thinking. Phillips translates verse 28a, "They considered themselves too high and mighty to acknowledge God." Not once, not twice, but three times, Paul writes in Romans 1 that God gave them over to what they wanted. These sinners become "gross" sinners who live in gross darkness.

Paul lists in verses 29 through 32 the many evils that result in a life gripped by the cancer of degeneration: "Until they were filled—permeated and saturated—with every kind of unrighteousness, iniquity, grasping and covetous greed, (and) malice. (They were) full of envy and jealousy, murder, strife, deceit, and treachery, ill will and cruel ways. (They were) secret backbiters and gossipers, slanderers, hateful to and hating God, full of insolence, arrogance, (and) boasting; inventers of new forms of evil, disobedient and undutiful to parents. (They were) without understanding, conscienceless and faithless, heartless and loveless (and) merciless."

The guilty defendants are left speechless, angry, embarrassed and wanting to flee.

We can never be healed unless we recognize what God said about our lost condition. I remember the statement of a young man from New York City who came to Elim Bible Institute. After just three months at Elim, he came to me, his Dean of Students, and said, "I am leaving Elim." I was surprised as I had befriended him and sympathized with his sordid background. I answered him, "You have only been here three months. What's wrong?" He replied, "You are getting to know me too well, and I cannot let that happen." He left. He did not understand that God only highlights our past in order to bring complete cleansing and victory to us. How we sadden God when we walk away!

Chapter 6 THE "GOOD" SINNER

As one of the defendants you may be thinking, "Thank God, I am definitely not one of those 'gross' sinners. I would not think of doing what they do!" You may actually be a good citizen and a good community member, but being good in your own eyes does not hold up in God's courtroom. Paul begins chapter 2 of his Romans' letter with, "Therefore you have no excuse or defense or justification, O man, whoever you are who judges and condemns another." If you self-righteously say, "I think it is terrible the way those 'gross' sinners are acting," you have appointed yourself as judge over them. You have no legal right. "For in posing as judge *and* passing sentence on another, you condemn yourself, because you who judge are habitually practicing the very same things [that you censure and denounce]" (Rom. 2.1b).

First, Paul records that "gross" sinners stand accused, falling short of God's glory. Now he includes people who may not seem "so bad": "Since all have sinned and are falling short of the honor and glory which God bestows and receives" (Rom. 3.23). Everyone is a sinner and will be judged by God's perfect standard—Jesus, the Christ.

FIVE STANDARDS OF GOD'S JUDGMENT

In Romans chapter 2 Paul presents a fuller understanding of the five criteria by which God's rewards will be meted out. Paul is not discussing how God saves. God's judgment here does not refer to where a person will spend eternity. There is only one way to be saved from hell to heaven, and that is through believing in the precious blood of Jesus. According to Acts 4.12b, Jesus is the only way to heaven because there is "no other name under heaven given among men by *and* in which we must be saved."

What, then, are the five standards of judgment all about? For the believer, they cannot be about my sin—for I know He has taken away my judgment when He died on the Cross. God, the righteous Judge, will not judge sin twice. Jesus already paid the judgment for my sin. These five standards of judgment, then, are about something else and applied judiciously for all—believers and non-believers. Romans 2.2 says, "But we know that the judgment (adverse verdict, sentence) of God falls justly and in accordance with truth upon those who practice such things." This means all men and women will be judged by the same righteous standards.

Either I must take my judgment for falling short of the standards, or someone else must take the judgment for me. In the case of those who are saved, Jesus Christ has taken the judgment for our sin by His sacrifice on the cross.

THIS MEANS ALL MEN AND WOMEN WILL BE JUDGED BY THE SAME STANDARDS.

FIRST STANDARD: TRUTH

The prosecutor begins with **"Your Honor,** everyone must be judged by the *truth.*" Romans 2.2 (*KJV*) states: "But we are sure that the judgment of God is according to truth against them which commit such things." Moffatt's translation says, "We know the doom of God falls justly upon those who practice such vices." Griffith Thomas, in his book *St. Paul's Epistle to the Romans* says, "We know God's judgment will be according to truth and therefore absolutely impartial" (78).

When we study the second chapter of Romans, we can compare it with 1 Corinthians 6.9-10 that states, "Do you not know that the unrighteous and the wrongdoers will not inherit or have any share in the Kingdom of God? Do not be deceived (misled); neither the impure and immoral, nor idolaters, nor adulterers, nor those who participate in homosexuality, Nor cheats—swindlers and thieves; nor greedy graspers, nor drunkards, nor foulmouthed revilers and slanderers, nor extortioners and robbers will inherit or have any share in the Kingdom of God."

Verse 11 of 1 Corinthians 6 continues on to say, "And such some of you were (once). But you were washed clean [purified by a complete atonement for sin and made free from the guilt of sin]; and you were consecrated (set apart, hallowed); and you were justified (pronounced righteous, by trust) in the name of the Lord Jesus Christ and in the (Holy) Spirit of our God." In other words, all people are judged by the same standard of God's truth. Jesus said, "I am the way, the truth and the life" (Jn. 14.6). He is truth. Unbelievers choose to take the judgment upon themselves; believers choose to accept Jesus Christ to take their judgment (Jn. 3.15-18). We who believe have a wonderful salvation! We may have been among the "gross" sinners or the "good" sinners, but Jesus has taken the judgment for us. Romans chapters 4 through 8 further explain how Jesus has taken our place of judgment.

SECOND STANDARD: DEEDS

The second standard of God's judgment is found in Romans 2.6-10 (*KJV*): "Who will render to every man *according to his deeds:* To them who by patient continuance in well doing seek for glory and honour and immortality, eternal life: But unto them that are contentious, and do not obey the truth, but obey unrighteousness, indignation and wrath, Tribulation and anguish, upon every soul of man that doeth evil, of the Jew first, and also of the Gentile; But glory, honour, and peace, to every man that worketh good, to the Jew first, and also to the Gentile."

God will judge all of us according to our deeds. Someone

best way possible, will not be judged as severely as someone who knew the Lord and turned his or her back on the Lord in rejection because this person knew the Light but rejected the Light. His judgment will come with many stripes. Remember, this is a judgment for "rewards," not to purchase salvation!

Believers will not have equal positions in heaven. There will always be an eternal assurance that we have been saved only by His grace; however, there is coming a day when even those who are saved by grace will give an account of how they obeyed the light they had. When we stand before God will He say, "Well done, thou good and faithful servant . . . enter thou into the joy of thy Lord" (Matt. 25.21)?

FIFTH STANDARD: SECRET MOTIVES

Romans 2.16 reveals, "On that day when, as my Gospel proclaims, God by Jesus Christ will judge men in regard to the things which they conceal—their hidden thoughts." That is, people will be judged according to their *motives*. According to motive is the final standard that applies to all people.

One act of righteousness is spoken of in Matthew 6. It is secret giving. Why secret? In order that your heavenly Father may reward you openly at a later date. Anonymous giving has no motive other than benefiting another. If you announce your giving, you announce your motive—the praise of man. When you seek the praise of man in this life, you forfeit your eternal reward. Your final reward will be for those acts for which you have not already received a credit. Everything you do for God, no matter how big or small, will receive its final reward based on the motive for your action.

EVERYTHING YOU DO FOR GOD,
NO MATTER HOW BIG OR SMALL,
WILL RECEIVE ITS FINAL REWARD
BASED ON THE MOTIVE FOR YOUR ACTION.

Chapter 7
THE "RELIGIOUS" SINNER

The prosecutor reviews the case thus far, "First there were the 'gross' sinners, and next the 'good' sinners. Both groups of sinners had righteousness that added up to a big, fat zero." The accuser now addresses the third and final group: the "religious" sinners.

"Ladies and gentlemen, do you think 'religious' sinners score better with true righteousness? No! When you rely on your measly religious performance, you too score a big zero in righteousness. It may be easy for you to think 'gross' sinners score a zero, but you 'religious' sinners who rely on your religion instead of Christ, score the same. You profess what you do not possess and claim to be righteous by your own assessments of religious obligations and activities."

CLAIMS

The prosecutor swells with pride as he approaches the "religious" sinners and slowly presents his final argument:

> But if you bear the name of Jew, and rely upon the Law and pride yourselves in God and your relationship to Him, and know and understand His will and discerningly approve the better things and have a sense of what is vital, because you are instructed by the Law; and if you are confident, and you [yourself] are a guide to the blind, a light to those who are in darkness, and [that you are] a corrector of the foolish, a teacher of the childish, having in the Law the

> embodiment of knowledge and truth; Well then, you who teach others, do you not teach yourself? (Rom. 2.17-21)

Religious sinners claim they bear the right name. People in this group of sinners boast, "Well, I am a Baptist" or "I am a Catholic" or "I am a Pentecostal" or "I am a Jew." Persons in this group think they are okay because they go to the "right" church and do the "right" things. They appear decent and religious, but their church membership cannot save them. Only Christ saves.

Sinners in this group even boast of their special affiliation with God. They claim to have a monopoly on God and think they are the only ones who have a direct line to God. He is "our" God. This kind of exclusiveness sets in when a person tries to defend his or her own righteousness by religion.

Sinners in this group know the Law of God. They understand what God requires because they are ". . . instructed by the Law; and . . . having in the Law the embodiment of knowledge and truth . . ." (2.18-20). Knowing the Law shows them the revealed light of the will of God. However, knowing the Law does not equate to doing that Law. A "religious" sinner will claim salvation by professing religion without possessing true salvation. The knowledge seems clear in the mind but dead in the actions. They want others to do as they say, not as they do. The issue is not that they are wrong in their claims concerning the Law; they are wrong in their personal conduct. There is a disconnect between their claim and their conduct.

CONDUCT

God is looking at our conduct, which is the fruit of our belief. **"Your Honor,** religious sinners claim they are '. . . a guide to the blind, a light to those who are in darkness, and . . . a corrector of the foolish, a teacher of the childish . . .'" (Rom. 2.19-20).

The evidence in the case against all of mankind is mounting. One "religious" sinner vainly interrupts and claims, "But I am a person who is able to guide the blind. I have been a teacher to 'gross' sinners who have no Law. Furthermore, I feel so privileged to be a light to those who are in darkness and an instructor of these foolish people who are so immature."

Everyone else sitting in the courtroom sees the religious sinner's arrogance and false self-importance. The defense of himself is alarming because he is deceived into comparing himself to others he looks down upon.

Immediately the prosecution takes aim. "Well then, you who teach others, do you not teach yourself? While you teach against stealing, do you steal—take what does not really belong to you? You who say not to commit adultery, do you commit adultery—are you unchaste in action or in thought?" (Rom. 2.21-22a).

He continues with one eye staring intently at the Judge and the other at the religious sinner, "You who boast in the Law, do you dishonor God by breaking the Law . . . ? For, as it is written, The name of God is maligned and blasphemed among the Gentiles because of you!—The words to this effect are from [your own] Scriptures" (2.23-24).

The religious sinner remains motionless in the courtroom. He does not get it because he has a mental and spiritual blockage. If he does not even learn from what he teaches himself, how could he begin to learn from someone else? The religious attempts to defend himself eloquently, and may even quote from the early church fathers in both Hebrew and Greek, but this person does not measure up in his or her conduct to God's demands. The court recognizes that religious sinners do not possess what they profess. There is no righteousness apart from Jesus Christ.

CONDITION

The religious sinner has another problem. While he takes great pains to make sure he is physically circumcised, there is no corresponding spiritual circumcision. "The most intimate sign of belonging to God that we call circumcision does indeed mean something if you keep the Law. But if you flout the Law you are to all intents and purposes uncircumcising yourself!" (*J.B. Phillips,* Rom. 2.25). The outward sign of circumcision is just that—an outward sign pointing to a deeper inner meaning. The spiritual meaning is that God has cut away the flesh in a person's heart in order to remove the hindrances to fulfilling the Law. For the religious sinner there is no connection between the outward sign of circumcision and the inner reality of a circumcised heart with corresponding behavior! Although we may view ourselves as pretty good, God the Judge sees us in the courtroom as defenseless, lost sinners without Christ.

COMPARED

Who exactly is a Jew as defined by the apostle Paul? Read the following written by the apostle in Romans 2.25-29:

> Circumcision does indeed profit if you keep the Law; but if you habitually transgress the Law; your circumcision is made uncircumcision. So, if a man who is uncircumcised keeps the requirements of the Law, will not his uncircumcision be credited to him [as equivalent to] circumcision? Then those who are physically uncircumcised but keep the Law will condemn you who, although you have the code in writing and have circumcision, break the Law. For he is not a [real] Jew who is only one outwardly and publicly, nor is [true] circumcision something external and physical. But he is a Jew who is one inwardly, and [true] circumcision is of the heart, a spiritual and not a literal [matter]. His praise is not from men but from God.

How does Paul's definition of a real Jew compare to a religious sinner's assessment of himself or herself? Paul explains that a Jew is someone who actually keeps the Law. Even though the Gentiles do not have the advantage of being entrusted with the Commandments, their right conduct will be credited as equivalent to circumcision. The religious sinner thinks that physical circumcision is an end in itself. Paul claims a "true" Jew is not someone born naturally a Jew, but someone who is born again spiritually by faith through a personal relationship with the Jewish Jesus—the Messiah.

Scripture offers additional insight into this truth in the book of Galatians. Abraham and Jesus are the main characters of Galatians chapter 3. The one received the promise; the other was the fulfillment of the promise.

> But the Law does not rest on faith [does not require faith, has nothing to do with faith], for it itself says, He who does them [the things prescribed by the Law] shall live by them [not by faith]. Christ purchased our freedom [redeeming us] from the curse (doom) of the Law [and its condemnation] by [Himself] becoming a curse for us, for it is written [in the Scriptures], Cursed is everyone who hangs on a tree (is crucified); To the end that through [their receiving] Christ Jesus, the blessing [promised] to Abraham might come upon the Gentiles, so that we through faith might [all] receive [the realization of] the promise of the [Holy] Spirit. (Gal. 3.12-14)

God requires faith first, not Law. The requirement by which God makes any one of us acceptable is our faith in Christ. We are not acceptable through the Law or being part of a certain group of people. By faith we all are partakers of the same promise of the Holy Spirit, Who becomes our spiritual sign and seal.

God requires faith first, not Law.

In Galatians the spiritual promises are given to Abraham and his Seed, not to Abraham and his seeds:

> Now the promises (covenants, agreements) were decreed and made to Abraham and his Seed (his Offspring, his Heir). He (God) does not say, And to seeds (descendants, Heirs), as if referring to many persons; but, And to your Seed (your Descendant, your Heir), obviously referring to one individual, Who is [none other than] Christ, the Messiah. (Gal. 3.16)

God's promise was given to ". . . Abraham and his Seed (his Offspring, his Heir)." The word *Seed* is capitalized because it is a proper noun. The word *Seed* has no letter "s" on the end of it because it is singular referring to just one Person. Then the author of Galatians states the obvious, ". . . Who is [none other than] Christ, the Messiah." In case anyone misses the capital S and singular form of the word *Seed*, he comes right out and states to whom he is referring—"none other than Jesus Christ."

Abraham became God's chosen person because he exhibited faith in God and obeyed Him. For people of faith Abraham is their father. In the natural Abraham had children, but only those who share Abraham's faith DNA are the true people of God.

Those who are naturally born Jews and those who are naturally born Gentiles have equal opportunity of becoming a "true Jew." Galatians confirms this truth by explaining the promise is granted supernaturally to those who put their faith in the Seed—Jesus Christ. God has children but no grandchildren. Natural Jews and Gentiles have equal value and opportunity with God. Paul expounds further in chapters 9 through 11 of his Romans letter.

CORRECTED

The first few verses of Romans 3 could be titled "Echoes from the Synagogue." After Paul's uncommon definition of a true Jew in chapter 2, there are bound to be repercussions. Paul immediately addresses any possible misunderstanding or imbalance of interpretation of his explanation. "Then what advantage remains to the Jew?—How is he favored? Or what is the value or benefit of circumcision?" (Rom. 3.1). There it is. Paul answers the first logical rebuttal question with, "Much in every way." He continues on by naming a specific example of an advantage: "To begin with, to the Jews were entrusted the oracles (the brief communications, the intentions, the utterances) of God" (Rom. 3.2). One advantage of being born a natural Jew is that they were the ones to whom the Ten Commandments were given.

Paul does not stop with only one advantage. In chapter 9 he expounds further, concluding with the advantage of being the people through whom the Messiah, the Son of God, was born.

> For they are Israelites, and to them belong God's adoption [as a nation] and the glorious (Shekinah) Presence. With them were the special covenants made, to them was the Law given. To them [the temple] worship was revealed and [God's own] promises announced. To them belong the patriarchs, and as far as His natural descent was concerned from them is the Christ, Who is exalted and supreme over all, God, blessed forever! Amen—so let it be. (Rom. 9.4-5)

However, the fact that people have "advantages" does not mean they do not need salvation.

The religious sinner is still trying to defend himself against staggering evidence. He continues rehearsing his religious duties, "But, I go to synagogue faithfully, and I wear the badge of circumcision. I am a leader of the blind and a light to those who never heard of the Ten Commandments. I have done a lot of good deeds for mankind." This religious sinner does not know when to be quiet! This sinner stands just as guilty as the gross sinner, because he believes salvation comes by religion and good works.

There is no merit in trying to save yourself! Whether we are lost "gross" sinners, lost "good" sinners, or lost "religious" sinners,

God wants us to receive the promise of life given through the Seed, Jesus Christ. That promise comes only by faith.

So then, if natural Jews have the advantage of being given the oracles of God (Ten Commandments) and some still do not believe in the Seed who came through them, what then? Are the promises of God of no effect anymore? Paul answers that question in verse 4: "By no means! Let God be found true though every human being be false and a liar, as it is written, That You many be justified and shown to be upright in what You say, and prevail when You are judged [by sinful man]." God always keeps His promises.

In Genesis 12.2 God promised to bless Abraham in order that Abraham would bless others. How, then, will God keep His promise that He will use natural Jews to bless others? Paul specifically answers this apparent contradiction in Romans 11. "So too at the present time there is a remnant (a small believing minority)" (Rom. 11.5a). Romans chapters 9 through 11 will shed more light about the believing Jewish remnant through whom God will fulfill His promise He made to father Abraham.

There is no national or ethnic salvation, and every person must personally believe in Jesus Christ. Salvation is always personal. If we believe in our hearts and confess with our mouths, we shall be saved (see Rom. 10.9). A Jew or Gentile is born again *only* by the cleansing blood of Jesus Christ. God's requirement is based on faith in His Son's sacrifice, not in natural descent or in religious affiliation.

WE CANNOT JUSTIFY OURSELVES

Now that the prosecutor has established that "all have sinned," someone might argue, "But if our unrighteousness thus establishes and exhibits the righteousness of God, what shall we say? That God is unjust and wrong to inflict His wrath upon us [Jews]? I speak in a [purely] human way" (Rom. 3.5). If my being bad makes God look good, then my "badness" is ,in a way, helping God to look good. Isn't that right? Paul responds in verse 6: "By no means!" or "God forbid: for then how shall God judge the world?" (*KJV*). Furthermore someone may argue, "... If through my falsehood God's integrity is magnified ... why am I still judged as a sinner? And why should we not do evil that good may come?" (7-8). This argument is a last resort attempt for a sinner to try to justify his or her condition. Sinners even accused Paul and his associates of teaching this falsehood: "as some slanderously charge us with teaching" (8b). Can you see how foolish the human mind is in its arguments to try to justify its lost position?

Chapter 8
THREE WITNESSES

The prosecution now calls in three trustworthy "witnesses" to take the stand against the defendants. Romans 3.10-12 reveals the detailed documentation of the first witness—a *historian*—who claims all defendants have always been bad, even if they do not remember being bad. The historian reminds them of their worthless acts, some recorded centuries ago by King David (Psalm 14.2,3). The next witness is a *doctor* whose diagnosis Paul records in Romans 3.13-16: "Their throat is a yawning grave; they use their tongues to deceive—to mislead and to deal treacherously. The venom of asps is beneath their lips. Their mouth is full of cursing and bitterness. Their feet are swift to shed blood. Destruction (as it dashes them to pieces) and misery mark their ways." The final witness, *a lower court judge,* declares, "I have more bad news about these humans. I have witnessed and heard from their own mouths that there is no reverential fear of God before their eyes." The apostle Paul notes these statements in chapter 3, verses 17 through 18, of his letter.

The supreme Judge slowly turns toward the self-represented defense to discover whether or not there is any evidence to present in favor of the seemingly doomed defendants. There is no reply! Before the case began, the one representing himself rashly thought he would be able to defend not only himself, but also every accused person standing with him. Now, he remembers again the sign outside the courtroom silently reminding all who enter: "He who defends himself defends a fool."

The prosecution summarizes the wealth of condemning evidence in his closing argument. He finishes by proudly proclaiming the rule of Law: "Now we know that whatever the Law says, it says to those who are under the Law, that every mouth may be stopped and all the world may become guilty before God" (*NKJV*, Rom. 3.19).

The Judge reminds the court, "For no person will be justified —made righteous, acquitted, and judged acceptable—in His sight by observing the words prescribed by the Law" (Rom. 3.20).

The one who defends himself has no closing argument. So [men] are without excuse—altogether without any defense or justification. The whole world is silenced and held accountable to God (see Rom. 1.20 and 3.19).

VERDICT IN

The proof is in. The evidence is heard. A fair and balanced trial has occurred. The whole world regardless of race, skin color, language, religious affiliation, social class, lineage, and background stands accused—guilty before God. The gross sinner, the good sinner, and the religious sinner stand together totally guilty, helpless, and hopeless.

No one who has heard this case could still believe that any person could possibly be saved by inherent goodness. No one can hang onto any good thing about himself or herself because there is too much bad news. There is too much blatant and formerly secret evidence of guilt. We are totally lost. When we realize how totally lost we are, we can then begin to understand how totally found we can be. A just God cannot acquit a person with even a hundred millionth of a part of sin.

Every mouth is hushed before the Judge. An aura of impending judgment fills the room. The prosecutor has proven what he promised, and now addresses the Judge with his final statement. **"Your Honor,** they are without excuse (*KJV*, Rom. 1.20b). I rest my case!!"

The Supreme Judge, having heard all the arguments and deliberations, has made his final decision. The gavel falls. The verdict echoes through the ages—***guilty, guilty, guilty.***

PART III

A SURPRISING TURN OF EVENTS

Chapter 9
RIGHTEOUSNESS APART FROM THE LAW

Before the Judge has time to set a date for sentencing, a quiet Stranger quickly approaches the bench. **"Your Honor,** may I offer more evidence on behalf of all of these silenced defendants that will shed new light on your proclamation?"

"Of course," the smiling Judge responds.

Instead of presenting more accusing evidence against mankind, Jesus Christ now intervenes as the Defense Attorney in your favor!

NEW EVIDENCE PRESENTED BY JESUS CHRIST

The new evidence presented begins as such:

> But now the righteousness of God has been revealed independently and altogether apart from law, although actually it is attested by the Law and the prophets, namely, the righteousness of God which comes by believing with personal trust and confident reliance on Jesus Christ, the Messiah. [And it is meant] for all who believe. For there is no distinction, Since all have sinned and are falling short of the honor and glory which God bestows and receives. [All] are justified and made upright and in right standing with God, freely and gratuitously by His grace (His unmerited favor and mercy), through the redemption which is [provided] in Christ Jesus, Whom God put forward [before the eyes

> of all] as a mercy seat and propitiation by His blood—the cleansing and life-giving sacrifice of atonement and reconciliation—[to be received] through faith. This was to show God's righteousness, because in His divine forbearance He had passed over and ignored former sins without punishment. It was to demonstrate and prove at the present time (in the now season) that He Himself is righteous and that He justifies and accepts as righteous him who has [true] faith in Jesus. (Rom. 3.21-26)

In Romans 3.21-26 Paul records some of the most gracious, freeing words of the whole letter: "But now the righteousness of God has been revealed independently and altogether apart from Law." These words are hard for most of us to believe because before this, all we have heard is the prosecution's case based on the Law. The new basis for judgment presented by our new Defense, however, is grace. Grace frees us from the Law. This new evidence, which speaks in favor of sinful defendants, will change the outcome of this previously ominous case. The One Who died and is alive has now become our Advocate.

When Jesus came, He came to free us all from sin and the Law. Fulfilling the Law is no longer the access point to God. This means that no one is able to say, "I have kept the Ten Commandments from my youth" and hear God reply, "Oh, you are such a good boy. You should go to heaven." You and I will spend eternity with God only by His grace through faith in Jesus Christ.

THE RESURRECTION SIDE OF THE CROSS

The only defense we sinners have is the Cross of Jesus Christ. Paul boasted, "May it never be that I would boast, except in the cross of our Lord Jesus Christ" (Gal. 6.14). What we usually do when we accept God's gift of salvation into our lives is invite Him to take away all of our bad and sinful things—things like pride, lust, swearing, and stealing. We try to hang on to our self-assessed good points—things like our limited patience, our obscure caring, and whatever sins we have not committed. We still want to highlight the good in us. But God wants us to give him all of our "goodness" in exchange for His true goodness. We cannot know what true goodness is until we know the only One who is good.

THE ONLY DEFENSE WE SINNERS HAVE IS THE CROSS OF JESUS CHRIST.

SALVATION IS A GIFT

We cannot produce salvation but may receive it as God's free gift. None of our efforts affect our righteousness, for Christ provides righteousness apart from anything we do or do not do. However, when we receive Christ's righteousness, we will desire God's deeds. Good deeds do not lead us to righteousness; because we are righteous we do good deeds.

Some people mistakenly think that an outward posture makes them spiritual. For instance, people, no matter what language they speak, fold their hands or kneel when they pray. This is an international prayer posture. We may think this outward position makes a person spiritual and right with God. What Paul is saying in chapter 3 of Romans is that true spirituality is found only in being in Jesus Christ. When we are positioned in Him, everything we do becomes spiritual, when it is done in His Name.

YOU ARE RIGHTEOUS ONLY THROUGH THE PRECIOUS BLOOD OF JESUS CHRIST.

When you shovel snow or go for a walk or work in the kitchen, you are doing the living works of righteousness because you are doing them in Him. You are righteous only through the precious blood of Jesus Christ. An unbeliever with hands folded may be religious. A believer on the job is righteous. Our deeds do not make us righteous; Jesus Christ accomplishes righteous deeds through us who are clothed in His righteousness.

I remember seeing a small plaque hanging over a kitchen sink. It read: "Divine service will be conducted here three times daily." It is clear that when a believer carries out his or her daily duties "as unto the Lord" these deeds are a righteous offering of worship unto God.

Chapter 10
COURTROOM RIGHTEOUSNESS

Mankind has righteousness available to him right now," Jesus Christ our Lawyer summarizes His first point of defense. "These needy sinners will never be more righteous than they are the moment they believe with full faith, as born-again believers." This case is about making the unrighteous righteous—sinners into saints.

The second new piece of defensive evidence presented by Christ, our Counsel, is that His righteousness is available to defendants simply by believing. Jesus Christ is God the Father's final Word concerning righteousness: "Namely, the righteousness of God which comes by believing with personal trust and confident reliance on Jesus Christ (the Messiah)" (Rom. 3.22). There is no other standard of righteousness than Jesus Christ. Paul writes that Jesus, not the Law, is our righteousness (see 1 Cor. 1.30).

OUR RIGHTEOUSNESS COMES NOT BY ACHIEVING, BUT BY BELIEVING.

In order to be free, our righteousness must come from a different source than the Law and its demands. It does not come from what we do; it comes from in Whom we believe. Even failure should not hinder believers from enjoying His righteousness. He will convict His own of sin. Our righteousness comes not by achieving, but by believing. We are not made righteous by the works we perform, whether they are good or bad. We are made righteous independent of the Law. Righteousness is God's free gift given to those who have put their full trust in Jesus.

Righteousness is not given by degrees; we receive it fully when we believe. Either we are righteous, or we are not righteous. We cannot be half-righteous. This complete salvation is worked out by faith over a lifetime process of sanctification by the Holy Spirit's changing us into the image of His dear Son. This will be dealt with more fully in Romans, chapter 6.

The following is further evidence presented by our Defense Counsel as reported by Paul:

RIGHTEOUSNESS: A REVELATION

The believer's salvation has nothing to do with self-efforts; it has everything to do with God's mighty working power. This way the salvation we enjoy has been purposely designed by God to terminate our pride. You or I cannot say, "Well, God and I did it." We must not be like the flea in the story of the elephant and the flea that crossed a bridge. The flea was in the elephant's ear as the elephant thundered across the bridge. When the two arrived at the other side, the flea said to the elephant, "My, didn't we make that bridge shake?" The bridge shook and the flea assumed he had something to do with it. We echo the same silly flea assumptions when we say, "Well, I am saved because of my prayer life" or "It's my effort that accomplishes salvation." Not so! All salvation given by God comes out of what He has already done.

When you are saved, God does more than take you out of one place; He sets you into another. You are taken out of a sinful, condemned lifestyle and placed into a gracious, free lifestyle. However, you can take a person out of the world, but it is very difficult to take the world out of a person. This is why Paul urges us not to be ". . . conformed to this world: but be ye transformed by the renewing of your mind . . ." (*KJV*, Rom. 8.5 and 12.2). The book of Romans deals with every part of our being: body, soul, and spirit. There is an appeal for our bodies, ". . . make a decisive dedication of your bodies . . ." (Rom. 12:1). There is an appeal for your mind, ". . . But be transformed (changed) by the [entire] renewal of your mind . . ." (Rom. 12.2). There is an appeal for your spirit, ". . . fervent in spirit . . ." (*KJV*, Rom. 8.14-16 and 12.11). What Christ has done for you has made you totally His, and you can trust Him.

I remember when my brother and I took our lunches in brown paper bags to elementary school. Each day our lunches consisted of the same old, same old peanut butter and jelly sandwiches. As we sat in the lunchroom, our friend always came in with big sandwiches of turkey, beef, or ham. One day my brother and I suggested to our friend, "Let's exchange our lunches before we open the bags!" We agreed and eagerly exchanged his bag for both of ours. We expected the usual lunchmeat but, to our surprise, his mother had hurriedly squirted one glob of ketchup in the middle of two slices of bread—that was it—nothing more. When we come to Christ, we are never disappointed by His "lunch." We give Him our sickness; He gives us His health. We give Him our sin; He gives us His righteousness.

THE BATTER'S BOX

Allow me to illustrate what Christ has done for you through the analogy of a baseball game. Imagine yourself in a stadium playing for your favorite team. Imagine the diamond with the three bases and home plate. You are standing in the batter's box. You swing the bat around a few times, add a little rosin to your hands, and hit your foot a couple of times with the bat. You have the feeling you are going to hit a home run. The umpire hovers over you like a vulture. The pitcher winds up and throws a fastball. "Strike one!" The catcher crouches, greedy for strike two.

As an unbeliever this is the way one plays the game of life. The devil hovers over you shouting, "Strike one!" "Strike two!" "Strike three!" and "You're out! Hang it up. You tried your best. Get out of the game. You have failed again."

Life throws you a curve when you least expect it. You leave home base condemned and depressed. You thought being in control of life depended on your ability to perform, to be strong, to reason, and to defend yourself. Even the law of the game states, "Three strikes and you are out."

On the other hand, the day you are saved God takes you out of the rulebook of the Law and into His "game." The environment looks the same, the bases look the same, and your life at first does not look that much different on the surface. However, when you step into God's ballgame, you play by His new set of rules—His grace rules. The most significant new rule is that as long as you keep standing in the batter's box, you may keep swinging the bat until you hit a homer. It is no more "three strikes and you're out." In Christ you may carry on. It is impossible to strike out.

This new rule of grace makes no sense. How can the pitcher ever strike a person out? The pitcher can't. As long as you stay in the batter's box "in Christ," you can swing and miss high inside or low outside. The devil still shouts, "You're out!" because he uses the rulebook of the Law. He wants to distract, depress, and confuse you. However, in God's game you are a winner for you are in Christ. Your righteousness does not depend on hitting a homerun. Your righteousness depends on being in Christ by faith, receiving His saving grace. God wants to teach you the new "rules" of His game—guarantees of righteousness and victory. It is His gift to you—receive it.

Others may think walking with Christ is like walking a tightrope with no safety net below. You believe it is all up to you to balance yourself with a balance pole or else you will fall. You obsessively think, "I'm going to fall. I'm going to fall. I'm not going to make it." In Christ you have already made it. You are already righteous. You will never be more righteous than you are today! He is your safety net. Your right standing is in Christ. He does not require you to walk a tightrope with the strong winds of the enemy blowing against you. He calls you to rest in His everlasting safety net—His full salvation!

One day, during study, I heard the Spirit's voice say, "My road of salvation is wide enough to include margins for error." His road of salvation is not like the narrow white line down the center of a road. It is a full four-lane freeway heading straight to heaven. There is a berm on the right and a median on the left. You have room. You can run and dance. You are free!

RIGHTEOUSNESS AND THE OLD TESTAMENT

What did the Old Testament reveal about righteousness? Did it say anything or is this a totally new concept? Two of the Old Testament prophets had plenty to prophesy about divine righteousness. Isaiah and Jeremiah both refer to the coming righteousness several times:

> Drop down, ye heavens, from above, and let the skies pour down righteousness: let the earth open, and let them bring forth salvation, and let righteousness spring up together; I the LORD have created it. (*KJV*, Isa. 45.8)

> Behold, the days come, saith the LORD, that I will raise unto David a righteous Branch . . . and this is his name whereby he shall be called, THE LORD OUR RIGHTEOUSNESS. (*KJV*, Jer. 23.5-6)

See also Isaiah 45.24-25, 46.13, 51.5-6, 53.11, 56:1, 61:11, and 62.1-2; Jeremiah 33.15-16 (not an exhaustive list).

"Your Honor, the Old Testament prophets heralded the coming of righteousness. It had not appeared yet, but the prophets Isaiah and Jeremiah knew it was coming." Paul, in Romans 3.21, echoes the prophets' attestations, "But now the righteousness of God has been revealed independently and altogether apart from law, although actually it is attested by the Law and the prophets." The Law and prophets of the Old Testament attested it; it was fulfilled in Jesus Christ. Jesus is the exciting fulfillment of the prophets' amazing predictions.

Do you desire to live a victorious life? The key is faith in Christ and trust in His righteousness. Whistling a happy tune is not enough. Anything short of believing in Him will fail. You are not condemned in Jesus; you are grounded, anchored, defended, and safe in Him. He is the Rock of our salvation and our sure Defense.

RIGHTEOUSNESS AND FAITH

Our Defense goes on to say, "If righteousness could come by Law, then it would not be a gift. If righteousness comes by faith, then it must be a gift." Jesus Christ is the gift of righteousness. Paul assures us that Jesus is the righteous-bearing Messiah, "Even the righteousness of God which is by faith of Jesus Christ unto all . . ." (*KJV*, Rom. 3.22) and "Knowing that a man is not justified by the works of the law, but by the faith of Jesus Christ . . ." (*KJV*, Gal. 2.16).

We who believe have faith in Christ, and we live by the faith of Christ. Is it my faith or His faith? It is both. I am saved by receiving Christ's completed work for, "I am crucified with Christ: nevertheless I live; yet not I, but Christ liveth in me: and the life which I now live in the flesh I live by the faith of the Son of God, who loved me, and gave himself for me" (*KJV*, Gal. 2.20). If my access to God were dependent on my faith alone, sometimes I would "feel" Him and sometimes I would not. My faith can be fickle, so He pours in His faith when I am in doubt: "In whom we have boldness and access with confidence by the faith of him" (*KJV*, Eph. 3.12).

WE WHO BELIEVE HAVE FAITH IN CHRIST, AND WE LIVE BY THE FAITH OF CHRIST.

Faith is a gift. If we could pay even two cents for our salvation, then it would no longer be a gift but a fantastic bargain! Everything that comes from God is a gift—the gift of salvation, the gift of the Holy Spirit, the gift of righteousness, and the gift of faith, to mention a few. There is nothing you can do to earn, to deserve, or to pay for a gift. A true gift is freely given.

A person is born again only through faith in Christ, not by faith in faith. Think about it, how much did you have to do with your natural birth? Now think about your spiritual life. Only faith in Jesus Christ makes a person born again. Faith in Christ is not a favorable opinion about Jesus Christ; it is a total commitment to and reliance on Him. Saving faith is not general; it is specific between you and the Person of Jesus Christ. Faith is our acceptance of God's offer of Himself in love and grace through Jesus Christ: "according to the degree of faith apportioned by God to him" (Rom. 12.3b).

RIGHTEOUSNESS WITHOUT HUMAN DISTINCTION

Romans 3.22-23 (*KJV*) defines righteousness as ". . . unto all, and upon all them that believe: for there is no difference: for all have sinned, and come short of the glory of God." This is the crux of our defense: all have sinned according to the Law, but the final verdict will be based not on law but on grace.

RIGHTEOUSNESS RECEIVED

Since all have sinned, all may be ". . . justified freely by his grace through the redemption that is in Christ Jesus" (*KJV*, Rom. 3.24). Jesus is an equal opportunity Savior. I am justified—"made just-as-if-I'd never done it." Faith in Jesus justifies a person so completely that any record of wrongs is expunged. People may remind us, but God will not. There is nothing in God's record of us that would ever indicate the kind of sinful life we lived, for now our sins are washed away and we are justified as new creatures in Christ.

In the courtroom we, the human race, sat embarrassed because the whole world could see our flaws. The photographers and journalists crouched to be the first to publish all of the juicy evidence against us. Our relatives and friends heard stories of our past for the first time and now they, too, believe we had it coming to us. The following poem entitled "The Case Against the Human Race" explains our predicament well:

I sinned, and straightway, posthaste, Satan flew
Before the presence of the Most High God,
And made a railing accusation there. He said,
"This soul, this thing of clay and sod has sinned.
'Tis true that he has named thy Name but I demand
His death, for Thou has said,
'The soul that sinneth it shall die.'
Shall not thy sentence be fulfilled?
Is justice dead? Send now this wretched sinner to his doom.
What other thing can a righteous ruler do?"
And thus he did accuse me night and day,
And every word he spoke, oh God, was true . . .

But wait! Redeeming evidence has come into the courtroom. All the shame that troubled our guilty faces cries out for a pardon.

Then quickly one rose up from God's right hand
Before whose glory angels veiled their eyes:
He spoke, "Each jot and tittle of the law
Must be fulfilled: the guilty sinner dies.
But wait—suppose his guilt were all transferred
To Me, and that I paid his penalty!
Behold, My hand, My side, My feet.
One day I was made sin for him
And died that he might be presented faultless at Thy throne!"
And Satan flew away. Full well he knew,
That he could not prevail against such love,
For every word my dear Lord spoke was true!

— *Author Unknown*

There was One sitting in the heavenly court, at the right hand of the Father, who heard all of the condemning evidence. He rose up and interjected, "Their guilt demands justice for 'Each jot and tittle of the law must be fulfilled: the guilty sinner dies.' But wait . . . ." Romans chapters 4 through 8 unfold the rest of the case with insights into the price He personally paid to purchase our pardon.

RIGHTEOUSNESS: ATTRIBUTE AND GIFT

In the same courtroom where we were openly proven guilty, a judicious way for us to be declared free is introduced. This right standing in God's eyes cannot be earned; it is a free gift! A gift is not received because a person feels that he or she deserves a gift. Gifts are received on the basis of trust and gratitude. God gifts us with His unconditional, unchanging, and eternal love.

Some years ago as I was teaching a class on the book of Romans, one of my students caught the truth of this courtroom scene and wrote the following poem:

All heaven and earth assembled, one dark and hopeless day;
As mankind stood before the judge, with nothing left to say.
There was a case against him, his verdict would be sealed,
Guilty, without excuse, and no further appeal.
Silent, helpless, groping there man stood,
All evidence had proven there was none that doeth good.
His case had been presented, his verdict was now sealed,
Guilty, without excuse, and no further appeal.

Falling to his face in shame, with not a word to say,
Man disclaimed the living God and followed his own way.
Before the case was laid to rest all gathered that day knew,
Man was guilty, without excuse,
there was nothing he could do.

Fallen, prostrate there man lay, beneath the righteous chair,
Awaiting the dark sentence, he was now about to hear.
The evidence was conclusive, the courtroom held their breath,
When the judge slammed down his gavel,
the sentence would be death.

But to everyone's amazement, the gavel did not fall;
But One stood up with nail-scarred hands and said,
"I paid it *all*."
I who knew no sin at all, became sin for thee,
And he held those nail-scarred hands outstretched,
for all the court to see.

All heaven and earth broke forth in praise,
that new and glorious day,
As mankind stood before the judge, with nothing left to pay.
The case against him was dismissed, his pardon ever sealed,
Forgiven, loved, accepted in Christ his one appeal.

In man's darkest hour, Jesus came to embrace,
The utter degradation of Adam's helpless race,
My Lord who knew no sin at all, became sin for me,
That in His righteousness I'd stand for all eternity.
— *Gwyn Thompson Eppard*

Isn't that powerful? Remember, mankind is guilty. Even religious sinners are inherently guilty. All who do not receive His saving grace will be sentenced to hell—an outer darkness prepared for Satan and his angels. There is no way out! We cannot defend ourselves. The verdict has been given. We are guilty and awaiting the sentence to be carried out if we do not accept Jesus Christ's free gift of salvation.

We are all tempted to try and defend ourselves. We have strong, inborn defense mechanisms. However, whenever we foolishly attempt to defend ourselves, we compromise the full acceptance of Christ's righteous gift. Relax and receive. God wants us to receive the joy of our salvation! He has saved us to set us free—free to laugh, free to cry, and free to fall or stand when we are born again into His family.

PART IV

THE BELIEVER'S DEFENSE CONTINUED

Chapter 11
COURTROOM: NEW EVIDENCE

The Defense Counsel continues, **"Your Honor,** I submit new evidence to this court." The room is hushed. Each defendant sits amazed, unable to speak a word, silenced by divine decree. "Who in the world is this Counselor of ours?" each wonders to himself.

One standing in the courtroom reaches out His nail-scarred hands as the new evidence introduced before the Judge. **"Your Honor,"** He gently whispers. "My scarred body is the new evidence presented on behalf of these guilty sinners."

The Lawyer opens up the Bible that was used to swear the truth, the whole truth, and nothing but the truth and looks down as he reads aloud the words of Romans 3.24-26:

> We "are justified freely by His grace through the redemption that came by Christ Jesus. God presented Him as a sacrifice of atonement, through faith in His blood. He did this to demonstrate His justice, because of his forebearance He had left the sins committed beforehand unpunished—He did it to demonstrate His justice at the present time, so as to be just and the one who justifies those who have faith in Jesus." (*NIV*)

Jesus Christ is the propitiation (mercy seat) for mankind. In God's judicial court, His blood made atonement and reconciliation for us.

PROPITIATION FOR ALL TIME

The Defense seizes the opportunity and declares, **"Your Honor,** this evidence proves Your grace alone makes Your righteousness available. This amazing new evidence fulfills the Law. In addition, Hebrews 9.15 confirms the most recent oral argument: '[Christ, the Messiah] is therefore the Negotiator and Mediator of an [entirely] new agreement (testament, covenant), so that those who are called and offered it, may receive the fulfillment of the promised everlasting inheritance, since a death has taken place which rescues and delivers and redeems them from the transgressions committed under the [old], first agreement.'"

The letter to the Hebrews explains that sins committed in Old Testament times were permitted the blood of bulls and goats to cover those sins, but it could not take away sins. But when the righteous sacrifice, the Son of God, Jesus Christ, shed His blood for all of humanity, like a mighty ocean, He swept sin away (Heb. 9.12-14 and 10.4). He did not simply cover sin; He removed our sin. Do you believe? The Cross stands as the eternal sentinel bearing witness to the new evidence presented on your behalf. This evidence is efficacious, having meaning and power for those under the Old Testament as well as the New.

You and I are free because Jesus Christ's blood, shed on the Cross, speaks for us. It says, "If we confess our sins, he is faithful and just to forgive us *our* sins, and to cleanse us from all unrighteousness" (1 Jn. 1.9). You and I are legally freed when we accept and believe in Jesus Christ, who took our sin on His cross. Part of Charles Wesley's old hymn "Arise, My Soul, Arise" puts it this way: "Five bleeding wounds He bears; received on Calvary. They pour effectual prayers, they gladly plead for me; forgive him oh, forgive, they cry, nor let that ransomed sinner die." One New Testament book says it like this, "You must know (recognize) that you were redeemed (ransomed) from the useless (fruitless) way of living inherited by tradition from [your] forefathers, not with corruptible things [such as] silver and gold, But [you were purchased] with the precious blood of Christ, the Messiah" (1 Pet. 1.18-19a).

When Admiral Byrd explored the South Pole, he never wandered out of sight of his markers. He walked until he could barely see his camp, and then he placed a stick in the ground as a marker. He continued walking, placing a stick in the ground each time he could just see the last stick. This way he did not get lost. We too have a stick in the ground, a marker, to show the way. Our stick is the Cross of Jesus Christ. Whenever we lose our way, we just need to look back to the Cross. Better yet, live in its shadow.

JUSTICE AND THE JUSTIFIER

God revealed His mystery, hidden for ages, when He revealed Jesus as our heavenly sacrifice and Advocate. Jesus Christ is the revelation of God the Father's divine wisdom. God is always just—He can be no other; however, the sins of humanity scream for mercy not justice. How does God, then, satisfy His own perfect justice? His love sent His one and only Son to pay the penalty and become the Justifier. "To declare, I say, at this time his righteousness: that he might be just, and the justifier of him which believeth in Jesus" (*KJV*, Rom. 3.26). So then, God is just (righteous), and God is the Justifier (the One who justifies). How could God possibly justify these wretched gross sinners, good sinners, and religious sinners? God is love (1 Jn. 4.8). God loves sinners. The demands of the Law are met by His love sacrifice, and we are justified and declared righteous when we accept His sacrifice.

Once there was a very young boy who violated a serious household rule. His parents considered carefully the consequences of his punishment and determined that the boy would be deprived of his room and would sleep in the cold attic instead. That night, when everyone went to bed, the concerned parents tossed and turned in sleepless unrest. Finally, the father got up out of bed, went to the cold attic to sleep, and sent his small son down to sleep with his mother. It would have been easier on the father to forego the punishment, but then justice would not have been served. It would have been easier on the father to issue another, less severe punishment, but that would have sent the wrong message to the boy. The father (mindful of justice but motivated by love) decided to trade the boy's punishment for his own comfort instead.

So it is with our heavenly Father and His Son Jesus. After thousands of years of man making sacrifices to God in order to try to satisfy His justice for sins, God sent His Son to make the ultimate sacrifice "once and for all." God was willing to make a trade—the sacrifice of His Son for our freedom. The Hebrew word for sacrifice means, "to draw near." It was by God's sacrifice of His Son that we now are able to draw near to God! God really loves sinners.

IT WAS BY GOD'S SACRIFICE OF HIS SON THAT WE NOW DRAW NEAR TO GOD!

We are justified by His grace, not our works. We are justified by receiving His finished work by faith, not by works of the Law. We are justified by faith that leads to works, not works that lead to faith. The Justifier justifies us because love paid the price!

INTRODUCTION OF FAITH

In Romans chapter 3 the apostle Paul presents a series of questions and answers to form the "introduction of faith." The first question is: "Then what becomes of [our] pride and [our] boasting?" (27a). What happens to the human pride of achievement? Has our failure to keep the Law killed it? Not at all, rather we are now judged righteous on a different basis, by a different standard. It is by believing instead of by achieving. Now a man or woman is justified before God by the fact of faith in Jesus Christ alone, not by what he or she manages to achieve under the Law. Believing gives you a new identity as a child of God in His family.

Righteousness by faith excludes boasting. The apostle Paul's "boasting" was in the Cross of Christ alone (Gal. 6.14). When we boast in the Cross, we exalt Christ instead of ourselves. True faith in God's ability removes any credit we might take for what is being accomplished in and through us by the Holy Spirit.

Paul's second question is found in verse 29: "Do you suppose God is the God of the Jews alone? Is he not the God of Gentiles also?" (*NEB*). The lawyer in Paul anticipates this sort of question, and he quickly offers the following answer: "Certainly, of Gentiles also, if it be true that God is one. And he will therefore justify both the circumcised in virtue of their faith, and the uncircumcised through their faith. Does that mean we are using faith to undermine the law? By no means; we are placing law itself on a firmer footing" (*NEB*).

Whether you were born a Jew or a Gentile, you can be justified by only faith. No one can boast, "I am a Jew, therefore I am justified before God" or "I am a Gentile, therefore I am justified before God." Our justification is not racial; it is by faith. Righteousness by faith excludes all racial distinctions.

Paul anticipates the next logical question, "Do we then by [this] faith make the Law of no effect, overthrow it or make it a dead letter?" (31a). His answer is emphatic, "Certainly not! On the contrary, we confirm and establish and uphold the Law" (31b). Faith recognizes the Law. In other words, when you and I could not fulfill the Law, the only way to keep the Law perfectly was for God to offer us righteousness apart from Law. The Law is still perfect. It is still the Word of God. However, in order for God to justify sinful humanity by the Law, He would have had to modify the Law, since it is impossible for us to obey it fully. Our justification, our righteousness is not a product of the Law.

Someone might ask, "Does the believer have to obey the Law?" You may have heard it said that believers are still under the Law because they should honor their fathers and mothers, should not commit adultery, should not covet, etc. Believers are no longer subject to the Law. Do not misunderstand, honoring your father and mother is still good and right, but we are unable to fulfill that Law fully. The Law is an inflexible, impossible, unattainable heavy burden.

Obedience has not been removed either. Now, instead of trying to obey the Law by our own strength, we through faith in Christ are empowered by the Spirit and, thus, fulfill the Law. It is no longer by our strength; it is by His strength. The difference between obedience to the Law and obedience to the Spirit is that the Law provides no power to obey. Fulfilling the law now becomes His promise to which our obedience is a love response.

FULFILLING THE LAW NOW BECOMES HIS PROMISE TO WHICH OUR OBEDIENCE IS A LOVE RESPONSE.

One day in my final year of Bible school, I was reading a book about Hosea the Prophet. Up to this time, I knew how to be active in the Lord's work because of my upbringing in the church. Somehow, in the back of my mind, I believed God loved me more if I served Him harder. In the middle of the night, while meditating on God's love, my room filled with His presence. I wept as He spoke to me, "Paul, if you turned your back on me and spit in my face, I could not love you less than I do now." This revelation that His love is not connected to my success or failure, freed me into His secure abiding love. My motive for serving Him changed at that moment from trying to earn His approval to embracing His love and acceptance.

Through faith the Ten Commandments become the Ten Promises. God the Father tells us, "Because I love you and freed you, I promise that you will have no other gods before Me. I hereby promise you will not murder or steal or covet." He frees us to respond to His voice, to love our neighbors, and to love God. "It was for freedom that Christ has set us free" (*NASB*, Gal. 5.1). The books of James and Romans balance Law and liberty. Those who think that the liberty of Romans sets them free to do anything need to understand the book of James. Those who are in bondage to the Law need to understand the book of Romans and Galatians.

"Thou shalt not kill."

"Because you are my child, I God promise you, 'Thou shalt not kill.'"

The Old Testament, which includes the Ten Commandments, is the Old Covenant. The New Testament, which begins with the life and death of Christ, is the New Covenant. The Old Covenant required two parties to agree to do their parts. If the people chosen would do their part, God would do His part—it was conditional. On the other hand, the New Covenant requires only one party to act and to bless us "with all spiritual blessings" through His Son Jesus Christ.

Our inability to keep the Law is not due to the weakness of the Law, it is due to the weakness of our flesh. "For what the law could not do, in that it was weak through the flesh . . ." (*KJV*, Rom. 8.3). The power to obey the Law must be found in the person who receives the Law. The Law became weak because the people who received it had no power to keep it. In Christ the power to fulfill the requirements of the Law is with the Promiser, not in the weak human receivers. When the Law demanded death to the one who violated its requirements, Jesus by His sacrificial death fulfilled its requirements.

Let us apply the most important Commandment to our everyday lives: "Thou shalt love the Lord thy God with all thy heart, and with all thy soul and with all thy mind" (Matt. 22.37). This is a command, and we struggle to obey it. I struggle because I cannot muster up enough strength in my flesh every moment of every day to love God absolutely. No worry. I hear God's voice promise, "Because you are my child, I promise that you will 'love the Lord thy God with all thy heart, and with all thy soul and with all thy mind.'" The Law's demands are now met by His promise to me. The reason I do not steal, covet, or commit adultery is that His promise is working through me. The power is in the Promiser not in the promisee!

The one who has received the promise receives it with the power of the Promiser. "But as many as received him, to them gave he power to become the sons of God" (*KJV*, Jn. 1.12a). When God turns the Law into a believer's promise, He takes the responsibility to fulfill it. He says, "And I will give them one heart, and I will put a new spirit within you; and I will take the stony heart out of their flesh, and will give them an heart of flesh" (*KJV*, Ezek. 11.19). Furthermore, He has already promised to write these things on the tablets of their hearts (see Jer. 31.33). When He writes His Laws upon the believers' hearts, He writes them as promises He intends to keep!

Thus far, three important points summarize the "introduction of faith": righteousness excludes boasting, righteousness by faith excludes racial distinctions, and righteousness by faith establishes the Law. As the defense of believers continues, a fourth important point will be addressed in the next chapter—righteousness by faith is true to history.

Chapter 12
COURTROOM: RIGHTEOUSNESS BY FAITH IS TRUE TO HISTORY

Romans chapter 4 continues the defense in your favor. Your Defense Attorney speaks, **"Your Honor,** I present to You historical evidence. The faith that sets men free has been with us since our Father Abraham. Faith is not a new concept or found only in the New Testament. This evidence is historically consistent."

THE FACT OF ABRAHAM'S FAITH

Jesus Christ, our Defense, continues, "Romans 4.1-12 recalls the faith of Abraham. Verse one begins the argument, '[BUT] if so, what shall we say about Abraham, our forefather humanly speaking? (How does this affect his position, and what was gained by him?)' I have already begun to establish that Abraham was justified by faith. It was a result of his believing, not his achieving. Verses 2 and 3 continue this thought, 'For if Abraham was justified (established as just by acquittal from guilt) by good works [that he did, then] he has grounds for boasting. But not before God! For what does the Scripture say? Abraham believed in (trusted in) God, and it was credited to his account as righteousness.' **Your Honor** . . . ." Before the Defense finishes his sentence, the Judge raps his gavel.

"Quiet, please, in the court. There is too much commotion over this concept of justification by faith." The Judge then gives His nod for the Lawyer to continue.

"Your Honor, holy Scripture records that Abraham was justified by faith. Thus, justification by faith is true to history. It is an historical fact. How was Abraham justified? Romans 4.3 quotes Genesis 15.6: 'Abraham believed (trusted in) God, and it was credited to his account as righteousness—right living and right standing with God.'"

RIGHTEOUSNESS IS A GIFT

Everything we receive from God is a gift. "Every good and perfect gift is from above, and cometh down from the Father of lights . . ." (*KJV*, Jas. 1.17). Salvation is the gift of eternal life (Rom. 6.23). We are righteous because we have received the gift of righteousness (Rom. 5.17). There is nothing you or I can do to earn God's gift.

"Now to a laborer, his wages are not counted as a favor or a gift . . ." (Rom. 4.4). Did you ever work a job, when at the end of the week your boss said to you, "You've done so well this week, I want to give you a gift of 100 dollars for your week's hire?" If you work, you are paid your due wages. Your wage is the reward of your work. You cannot work or pay for a gift.

"But to one who not working [by Law], trusts (believes fully) in Him Who justifies the ungodly . . ." (4.5a). How can a just God possibly justify the ungodly? He is both just and the Justifier. He has not violated His justice; He Himself has fulfilled it. Paul continues, "Abraham's faith is credited to him as righteousness—the standing acceptable to God. Thus David congratulates the man and pronounces a blessing on him to whom God credits righteousness apart from the works he does" (5b-6).

"Your Honor," the Defense adds, "not only was Abraham justified by believing, but King David acknowledged that a man could be justified apart from his works. The next two verses refer to Psalm 32.1-2, written by King David: 'Blessed and happy and to be envied are those whose iniquities are forgiven and whose sins are covered up *and* completely buried. Blessed and happy and to be envied is the person of whose sin the Lord will take no account nor reckon it against him'"' (Rom. 4.7-8).

David wrote of something greater than our feelings—he wrote of our complete forgiveness. Paul says, "God was in Christ, reconciling the world unto himself, not imputing their trespasses unto them . . . " (*KJV*, 2 Cor. 5.19). God does not count our sins against us when we are in Christ. When confessed, our sin is not put in our ledger; rather, it is put in Jesus Christ's ledger. Jesus takes the debt of our sin and credits us with His abundant righteousness!

JESUS TAKES THE DEBT OF OUR SIN AND CREDITS US WITH HIS ABUNDANT RIGHTEOUSNESS!

When you understand God's forgiveness of debt, you are able to share the same gift with others. On the Cross, Christ prayed, "Father, forgive them." Paul prayed, "At my first answer no man stood with me, but all men forsook me: I pray God that it may not be laid to their charge" (*KJV*, 2 Tim. 4.16). Paul used an accounting term here, requesting that God not put the offense of abandonment into the ledgers of the offenders. Paul also spoke in defense of a slave when he urged, "If he hath wronged thee, or oweth thee aught, put that on mine account" (*KJV*, Philemon 1.18). Stephen shared God's gift when he pleaded for the sinners committing a life-threatening personal offense against him, "And he kneeled down, and cried with a loud voice, Lord, lay not this sin to their charge" (*KJV*, Acts 7.60). Is there someone for whom you could pray a similar prayer? If you have been forgiven, pass it on—it's a God thing!

"Your Honor, David and Abraham are historical witnesses who confirm the fact that a person can be justified by faith alone," the Defense concludes. "This is not a novel idea, but a proven principle with its roots in the Old Testament."

THE BASIS OF ABRAHAM'S RIGHTEOUSNESS

Paul now asks this question: "How then was righteousness credited [to him]? Was it before or after he had been circumcised? It was not after, but before he was circumcised" (Rom. 4.10). Abraham was justified some fourteen years before he was circumcised. He was justified *before* he offered his son Isaac, *before* he was circumcised, *before* he gave away his wealth, and *before* he began his journey from Ur of the Chaldeans. This time span is important in the history of justification. If Abraham's justification can be linked to the act of circumcision, then there is something a person must do to be justified. Circumcision would be the badge that makes us children of God.

Why, then, does James 2.21 state Abraham was justified by works when he offered up Isaac on the altar? Isn't that contradictory? Not at all. Abraham's work was an act of faith. Abraham was exercising the obedience that comes from faith. Abraham's action showed his faith was alive! Abraham still believed God's promise that through Isaac his seed would be counted. Abraham believed that God could raise Isaac from the dead. What was the proof he believed? The proof was his action at the altar of sacrifice on Mount Moriah. His faith responded obediently to God's word and produced the fruit of righteousness.

We wear ourselves out trying to keep our balance. We shift the weight of works and the weight of faith. We frantically move from one side to the other, desperately trying to keep our balance. The best way to keep a balance between faith and works is to allow the Lord to lead us into both faith and works.

Paul knew better than to treat circumcision as something meaningless. He was not trying to eliminate its true meaning, but to deal with the serious error of depending on it for justification. Some people had circumcision out of its Scriptural order. "It was *afterwards* that the sign of circumcision was given to him, as a seal upon that righteousness which

God was accounting to him as yet an uncircumcised man!" (*J.B. Phillips*, Rom. 4.11).

THE INHERITANCE OF ABRAHAM'S FAITH

It is very important that the divine promises of justification came to Abraham before he was circumcised. As far as the eternal promises of God go, there is no difference whether they go to Jew or to Gentile, slave or free, male or female. All who believe are the children of Abraham, for he is the "father of faith." To Abraham and his seed are given natural (by birth) and spiritual (by faith) promises, which in chapters 9 through 11 of Romans will be considered further.

MAN SEEKS GOD ON HIS OWN TERMS

Genesis 11 records the account of the Tower of Babel. This account indicates that man has a hunger to know God on his own terms. If we can just build a tower high enough to reach God, mankind thought, then we will be able to approach God based on our effort and "good" works.

God quickly put a stop to this building project. God will not allow sinful man to make his own ladder to God because then man could claim to be as God. We can never begin with faith in ourselves to reach God; we must begin by faith in God. True faith lays hold of something outside of oneself—a fixed point—the Cross of Christ, the anchor of faith! Stop trying to reach God by the things you do right! God has already made things right for you and by faith He will give them to you—believe and receive!

FAITH BY WHICH SALVATION IS RECEIVED

Genesis 11 marks the end of a futile attempt by mankind to make his own way to God. God scrambled man's language to stop the madness. Thousands of years later God redeemed this sad story when He poured out His Holy Spirit and gave man new languages: "And they were all filled—diffused throughout their souls—with the Holy Spirit and began to speak in other (different, foreign) languages, as the Spirit kept giving them clear and loud expression (in each tongue in appropriate words) . . . and they were astonished and bewildered, because each one heard them speaking in his own (particular) dialect" (Acts 2.4 and 6b). The Church was born.

At the beginning of chapter 12 of Genesis, Gods speaks personally out of heaven directly to Abraham: "Get thee out of thy country" (*KJV* Gen. 12.1a). God's presence reaches down and connects clearly with the faith of the individual. Faith is the instrument by which one receives personal salvation. Salvation comes to each person complete and whole by faith. To use the analogy of the body, faith in one way could be likened to the ear. The ear receives the sound but is not the sound. So faith is a "sixth sense" that is able to hear the voice of God and receive His gift of salvation. Paul uses Old Testament examples to strengthen Christ's case for faith in Romans, chapter 4. How will the gross sinner, the good sinner, and the religious sinner all be declared legally righteous? In the same way that Abraham of the Old Testament was declared righteous—by faith in God.

ABRAHAM REPRESENTS ALL MANKIND

While Abraham was in Ur of the Chaldeans, before he heard the voice of God and stepped out by faith, he was numbered just as any other person among mankind. But when he believed and obeyed, he began a new family. Abraham is not only the father of Isaac and Jacob; he is also the father of all who have faith. Abraham believed and obeyed. Thus, by faith and obedience, he was made righteous and the father of faith.

Back in the courtroom there remains a sinister onlooker who seethes at this new approach of the Defense. He hopes to find a way to turn the direction of the case back to works and the Law because he knows these defendants are guilty, and he enjoys airing his accusations publicly. Night and day, day and night, this accuser of the brethren schemes and plots his strategy against us.

He approaches the bench and turns to point his finger at the sinners. "'Tis true that he has named Thy Name but I demand His death, for Thou has said, 'The soul that sinneth it shall die.' You know these sinners did not pray enough today. They have not read their Bibles either. They spent all morning worrying about the circumstances in which they now find themselves. They have not fed the hungry, helped the helpless, or loved their enemies, as they should! They are guilty, guilty, guilty!"

The sinner who attempted to live by works is always under a cloud of condemnation because they know there is always more to do. The father of pride himself attacked any remnant of spirituality this person had left. His accusations confirmed there is nothing anyone can boast about or do to deserve salvation—not one thing—because all of mankind's works always miss the mark of God's perfection. Only Christ can set us free!

Chapter 13
INHERITANCE BY FAITH

Abraham received the badge of righteousness (circumcision) after he was already made righteous. He was a true believer. Faith is absolutely necessary in the Christian's relationship with God; circumcision is not. If a person depends on a rite in order to be justified, the rite compromises what Jesus Christ has already accomplished. What Christ has done is complete!

RIGHTEOUSNESS NOT BASED ON CIRCUMCISION

"It was afterward that the sign of circumcision was given to him, as a seal upon that righteousness which God was accounting to him as yet an uncircumcised man!" (*J.B. Phillips,* Rom. 4.11-12). A sign always points to that which already exists. People are baptized as a public sign they are already saved. Baptism is an outward sign signifying the burial of "the old nature" that is dead in Christ. You don't bury a person before they have died! To Abraham circumcision was the act that followed the fact. Abraham's inheritance was his by faith. "The ancient promise made to Abraham and his descendants, that they should eventually possess the world, was given not because of any achievements made through obedience to the Law, but because of righteousness which had its root in faith" (*J.B. Phillips,* Rom. 4.13).

ALTARS VS. TENTS

"It was faith that kept him journeying as a foreigner through to the land of promise, with no more home than the tents which he shared with Isaac and Jacob, co-heirs with him of the promise. For Abraham's eyes were looking forward to that city with solid foundations of which God himself is both architect and builder" (*J.B. Phillips,* Heb. 11.9-10). Abraham looked ahead to more than just a land of promise. He looked ahead to a larger possession—a heavenly city. Hallelujah!

A number of times in Genesis Abraham built an altar. An altar is something permanent. Each time Abraham also pitched his temporary tent. Many times we do it backwards—we pitch altars and build tents. We need to switch it around to build altars and pitch tents. Concentrate on the unseen eternal, not the visible temporal. Live for the timeless not the timely. Altars are the places where God meets us. They represent spiritual positions we access by faith. Altars are also places of sacrifice.

Abraham's nephew Lot did it backwards. He drew close to Abraham and said to himself, "It's a wonderful thing to have my Uncle Abe here; I like to be near him. I know the power of God is on him." While he was thinking this, he was also eyeing the well-watered plains of Jordan to scope out the best place for himself. He was building a tent and pitching an altar—always thinking about number one!

Abraham had only a spoken word from God; we have an entire Bible full of written promises from God and still we find them hard to believe. However, our forefathers of faith listed in Hebrews 11, including Abraham, believed God even though some ". . . died without actually receiving God's promises, though they had seen them at a distance, had hailed them as true and were quite convinced of their reality . . ." (*J.B. Phillips,* Heb. 11.13). These faithful followers looked forward, moving on toward the ultimate purposes of God by taking steps of faith. They were not tired settlers; they were bold pioneers.

ABRAHAM, THE FATHER OF FAITH

The defense's argument for faith continues with salvation as a matter of generosity on God's part and faith on man's part:

> For if, after all, they who pin their faith to keeping the Law were to inherit God's world, it would make nonsense of faith in God himself, and destroy the whole point of the promise. For we have already noted that the Law can produce no promise, only the threat of wrath to come. And, indeed if there were no Law the question of sin would not arise. The whole thing, then, is a matter of faith on man's part and generosity on God's. Your happiness, your righteousness, your standing before God depends on God. (*J.B. Phillips*, Rom. 4.14-16)

God gives the security of His own oath to all men who call upon His name by faith. Anyone with or without the advantage of the Law who has faith in Jesus Christ shares Abraham as a father because God said, ". . . but your name shall be Abraham (father of a multitude); for I have made you the father of many nations" (Gen. 17.5).

SALVATION, THEN, IS A MATTER OF GENEROSITY ON GOD'S PART AND FAITH ON MAN'S PART.

We are "in Christ" by His gift received by faith. At Pentecost, Jesus Christ poured out the power of the Holy Spirit on the Church (see Acts 2.32-33). Faith is a shadow in the Old Testament but is substance in the New Testament in the Person of Jesus Christ.

Chapter 14
THE NATURE OF ABRAHAM'S FAITH

Because faith is the basis of this new righteousness, Paul details Christ's defense in Romans 4.17-22. These verses focus on the nature of Abraham's faith. This kind of faith states, "I believe." First and foremost, it is a faith full of reverential recognition of who God really is.

REVERENTIAL RECOGNITION

Abraham recognized the power of the Person in whom he put his faith. He had the right reverential recognition although there were many idols in Abraham's heathen culture. He believed in the One and Only True God. Faith is only as strong as the object of that faith. For instance, you may have faith that your friend is going to buy you a new car when he doesn't have two pennies to rub together. You become disappointed in your expectation. You had great faith, but then the object of your faith did not produce that new car and your faith was weakened. The object of your faith was fallible. Abraham's faith was placed in the infallible God (see verse 17).

FAITH IS ONLY AS STRONG AS THE OBJECT OF THAT FAITH.

DIVINE CHARACTER

Second, it is a faith of divine character. God faith quickens the dead and calls things that are not as though they already were (17). His divine character is always good and desires to bring life.

GOD-FAITH QUICKENS THE DEAD AND CALLS THINGS THAT ARE NOT AS THOUGH THEY ALREADY WERE.

There is a divine quality to faith in God—it quickens dead people, people like you and me. The devil may whisper, "You can't say you're healed. You still have pain. You are a real hypocrite." You can reply, "It is, indeed, a fact that I have pain, but I believe I am healed." Faith is not the absence of pain or the denial of facts; faith is belief in the finished work of Calvary despite any contrary visible evidence. The eternal fact is that Christ's atonement has healed us, even when we do not feel or see it in the now. Healing does not come by feeling; it comes by faith. If God said it, His Word is truer than what you feel. When you have a faith like Abraham's, you can believe things that are not what they seem. This divine quality of speaking according to His will is what God requires and gives to believers. ". . . If we ask anything according to His will . . . we know that He hear us . . . we know that we have the petitions that we desired of him" (*KJV*, 1 Jn. 5.14-15).

The devil may remind you of your failures often, and you tend to quickly agree with him. But the faith that conquers failure is the faith that calls things that are not as though they were. Stop listening to the devil and your own thoughts. Do you really want to be healed? Jesus asked this same question to a sick man lying alongside a pool. If you are healed, it will put an end to complaining, begging, and an inferiority complex. Your whole life will change. Sometimes we have made begging and complaining to God a lifestyle. How desperate for change are you? Then call things that are not as though they were in accordance with God's word. That is what Abraham believed and acted on. He can make a beggar into a banker.

IN EVERY CIRCUMSTANCE

Third, Abraham's faith in God was in every circumstance: "[For Abraham, human reason for] hope being gone, hoped on in faith that he should become the father of many nations, as he had been promised" (Rom. 4.18a). Every human reason for hope was gone, yet Abraham "hoped on in faith" despite his hopeless circumstance. His faith was not in the circumstance, his faith was in God, Who could change the circumstances. He had faith in God when everything was impossible. Usually, we try every way to save ourselves. We mistakenly think, "If only I can find a way to do this myself; I will try a little harder." If so, we have not yet seen our salvation as humanly **impossible**. When we finally stop having faith in ourselves and put our faith in God, we will enjoy His divine life and gift of righteousness.

DEAL WITH "SENSE OBSTACLES"

Fourth, faith deals with "sense obstacles." When things stand in your way, God has given you senses in order to identify these things. Don't ignore them; deal with them. Faith deals with real and perceived problems.

There is a teaching abroad that encourages Christians to confess they are not sick even though the sickness is still there. This is unscriptural. If you are sick, say, "I am sick." This is not unbelief; this is a fact. Your circumstance is impossible. Abraham was not afraid to face the truth: "Without weakening in his faith, he faced the fact that his body was as good as dead—since he was about a hundred years old—and that Sarah's womb was also dead" (*NIV*, 19). Some people are afraid to acknowledge impossibilities. Abraham wasn't. He was old and impotent and unafraid to face it.

FIXED POSITION

Fifth, the kind of faith Abraham had looked like this: "No unbelief or distrust made him waver or doubtingly question concerning the promise of God, but he grew strong and was empowered by faith as he gave praise and glory to God . . ." (20). Abraham did not stagger.

Neither did he doubt. Instead, he gave glory to God. He fixed his faiths position directly on the One Who made the promise.

Abraham never turned away because he was "fully satisfied and assured that God was able and mighty to keep His word and to do what He had promised" (21). Do you believe God is able? Then fix your position on God. As a result, Abraham's faith ". . . was credited to him as righteousness—right standing with God" (22). It was not the size of his faith; it was the size of his God. It is the same for us. Faith the size of a mustard seed can move mountains or receive healing.

IT WAS NOT THE SIZE OF HIS FAITH; IT WAS THE SIZE OF HIS GOD.

True faith stands on the Word of God alone. I had this truth reinforced when I stood on a street corner in the middle of Nairobi, Kenya. I suddenly heard the words, "The city is mine, says the Lord." From this inspired *rhema* word, I claimed a parcel of land at a time when it was "impossible." God worked it out, and we ultimately received the land as a free gift from the city to All Nations Gospel Church, which stands there today. Faith is seeing God as bigger than the problem and His Word as more sure than any visible circumstances.

DIVINE CONFRONTATION

Finally, the remainder of chapter 4 explains the reason why all who believe in Jesus have access to a divine confrontation. Recall in verse 17 that Abraham stood "in the sight of God." Abraham knew he could stand right before God. He had no other human mediator. He could go straight to God with his questions. Job is one of many other Old Testament characters who also stood before God and addressed his complaints straight to God, not to people. We have the same access through Jesus Christ "Who was betrayed and put to death because of our misdeeds and was raised to secure our justification—our acquittal, and to make our account balance, absolving us from all guilt before God" (25). Perhaps we fail to implore Him because we prefer human sympathy to divine intervention? Human counsel is not divine forgiveness. He alone is able to even quicken the dead or forgive the sinner.

If it were not for the last two verses of chapter 4, the reader might begin to believe that miracles were great for Abraham, but no longer happen today for us. These last two verses connect you and me to all of chapter 4. These things were written down "for our sakes too" (24a). Righteousness "will be granted and accredited to us also who believe—trust in, adhere to and rely on—God Who raised Jesus our Lord from the dead" (24b).

Our faith must be focused on God and His specific revelation as we face all of life's problems. Confidence in yourself or others always undermines your faith in God. Paul writes again in Philippians 3.3, we ". . . have no confidence in the flesh." A general belief in God will not bring forgiveness for specific issues or sins in your life. You need personal belief in God for His forgiveness. Salvation and all that it encompasses is applied personally. You must believe in the specific revelation that God has given—namely, the death and resurrection of His Son Jesus Christ, for forgiveness of sin and eternal life.

The Old and New Testament emphasize the truth that the just shall live by faith (Rom. 1.17b).

"THE JUST SHALL LIVE BY FAITH"

As Martin Luther read and understood these few words, the transforming process began that changed his own thinking and the lives of millions. When you are "just" today, you live by faith, not by feeling. When we know the Word of God, we are not like a little sailboat floating on the peak of a wave in one moment and then drowning under water the next. When every kind of wind is blowing, these people are tracking up and down and back and forth rather than forward. Their lives are controlled by outside stimuli. For example, unstable people can react negatively when someone does not greet them or shake their hands. People who live their lives reacting to others and situations are emotionally unstable, immature, and blown about by every wind.

The internal Person of the Holy Spirit, however, controls those who live by faith. These people are more like submarines. When a storm comes and the waves increase, they are able to move forward, down, up or in any purposeful direction. The source of a submarine's movement is internal. This inner quality gives stability to live a consistent Christian life. When you and I fail to live by faith, we fall back into the "elephant ditch" of our lives as described in chapter 1 of this book. Remember, located in the basement are murky dirt and scary animals. There lives the tiger of lust, the lion of pride, and the cheetah of greed. Once these animals start fighting within, we feel the pain and pressure, and become out of control.

Every once in a while you go down into the basement with the whip of the law of God. Maybe you go there when you are at an evangelistic crusade with some fired-up evangelist. You endeavor to beat those animals into submission. "Down, down!" you say. They cower back into a corner. You think, "Thank God, I've won a big victory." Those fleshy beasts will rise again to attack you. However, Romans prescribes the way to deal with them so they won't ever return. It is no secret that God really wants them out of your life and you walking in His glorious victory.

The prescription verse in Romans is "The just shall live by faith" (*KJV*, 1.17b). This verse occurs four times in the Bible. The first time is in Habakkuk 2.4, right after the author finishes moaning and groaning about life's circumstances. Suddenly, the revelation of God comes to him and he writes, "the just shall live by his faith" (*KJV*). He has it.

This same verse is repeated three times in the New Testament. It appears first in Romans 1.17b. Romans emphasizes the **just** people because Romans is a book about justified people. It is the **just** who live by faith. It appears a second time in the New Testament in Galatians 3.11b. Here it states, "The just shall live by faith" (*KJV*). Galatians emphasizes how the justified people **live**. They **live** freely by faith. Finally, Hebrews 10.38a repeats the verse, "Now the just shall live by faith" (*KJV*). How do justified people live? Just people live freely by **faith**. The position of this Hebrews verse immediately precedes the greatest **faith** chapter in the entire Bible. Therefore, "The just" (Romans), "shall live" (Galatians), "by faith" (Hebrews). By faith, by faith, by faith—it is all by faith; it is not by feelings. Our salvation is not controlled by the winds of circumstances, but by an inner faith and confidence in God revealed to us by the Holy Spirit. The just shall live by faith. Amen.

Chapter 15
GOD'S FORGIVENESS THROUGH JESUS CHRIST

In Romans chapters 5, 6, and 7 our Defense lawyer builds His case as He deals with the specific revelation of God's forgiveness and redemption through Jesus Christ. Remember, the whole issue is a legal one. Our redemption is a legal fact: "THEREFORE, since we are justified—acquitted, declared righteous, and given a right standing with God—through faith" (Rom. 5:1a). This verse is in the present tense, not the future tense. It is all ours right now by faith. Remember, faith is the instrument that reaches up to receive His completed righteousness. As far as God is concerned (and He is the One that matters), He counts us righteous through the finished work of His Son Jesus Christ alone.

We receive gifts of peace and access when we are made righteous, according to Romans 5.1b-2a: "peace with God through our Lord Jesus Christ, the Messiah, the Anointed One. Through Him also we have [our] access (entrance, introduction) by faith into this grace."

OUR ACCESS THROUGH THE SON

We try to approach God like the filthy, dirty beggar boy who decided he wanted to visit his king. The boy walked from his little mud hut in the bush down into the city until he arrived at the king's palace. He knocked at the huge gate and tried to enter. Finally, an annoyed guard on duty came to him and said, "Hey, kid, what do you want?"

"I want to see the king," the frightened youth replied.

The guard laughed at him and sneered, "As you are, there is

God, but God desires to enlarge us so we will hold bucketfuls and barrelfuls of Him! The process of sanctification empties the vessel of clutter to make room for more of God.

When first saved, everything may seem to be going along well until we encounter another promise found in chapter 5, verse 3, "Moreover—let us also be full of joy now! Let us exult and triumph in our troubles and rejoice in our sufferings, knowing that pressure and affliction and hardship produce patient and unswerving endurance." Is your capacity for God only large enough that one "hallelujah" shout on Sunday causes you to bubble over with joy but on Monday you are dried up when trouble comes at work? Is your capacity for God still the size of a thimble? What you have is of God, but unless you allow the process of sanctification to work in your life, you will be depressed when trouble, suffering, pressure, affliction, and hardship come into your life. When you are "squeezed" what flows out, sour lemon juice or sweet apple cider? The problem is never with God; the problem is with us. Our lives look more like the inn at Bethlehem that had no room for Him than the simple, vacant, humble stable.

GOD'S ENLARGING PROCESS

God wants to bring us into a place of enlargement. The enlarging process begins with the faith of chapter 4, moves to rejoicing in hope (Rom. 5.2), and on into rejoicing in trouble, suffering, and hardship (3). The believer rejoices in hope and in tribulation. Why? Is it because believers are some kind of masochists? Absolutely not! It is because believers in Christ know that "tribulation worketh patience; And patience, experience; and experience, hope" (*KJV*, 3b-4). God's process of enlargement begins with hope and ends with more hope. Believers are able to glory in tribulation because it is only a means to an end—more hope. We have our eyes fixed on Jesus ". . . who for the joy set before him endured the cross . . ." (Heb. 12.2).

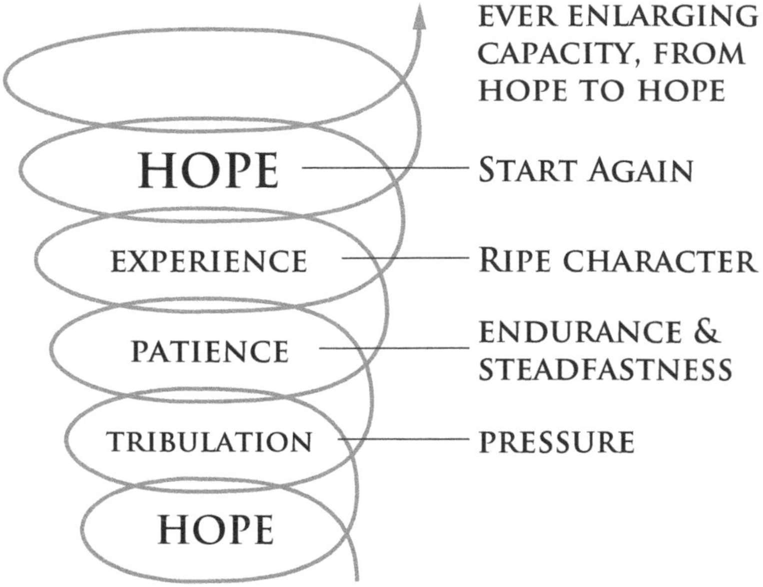

The word tribulation also means pressure. An increase in pressure produces an increase in hope. David confessed to God in Psalm 4.1 (*KJV*), "Thou hast enlarged me when I was in distress . . ." God is in the enlarging business. He desires to enlarge us. Pressures on the inside and pressures on the outside increase the vessel's capacity for knowing and showing God. We learn to put our faith in His unchanging character and not to rely on our feelings or to seek for quick answers.

Once there was a man who bought a pair of shoes and took them home before trying them on. When he realized the shoes were too tight, he returned them to the shoemaker to have them stretched. So the shoemaker placed a shoe-stretcher inside the shoe and turned it until the poor little shoe thought it would explode. But it didn't. It was stretched to be made useful. Every half hour, while the old cobbler was tapping away on other shoes, he reached over and gave another twist to the shoe-stretcher. Just when the shoe thought it could take no more and that surely the process was over, the cobbler added even more pressure with another turn.

GOD'S PROCESS OF ENLARGEMENT BEGINS WITH HOPE AND ENDS WITH MORE HOPE.

Similarly, when you and I feel we can take no more, God may add more pressure. He is enlarging our capacity to experience His glory. His increasing pressure is producing increasing patience or perseverance (Rom. 5.3). Some translations translate this word patience as "endurance." That means we gain endurance as a result of being steady under pressure. How much endurance do you have? Do you give up quickly on what God has promised? When we rely on easy times we are like a mountain bike cyclist traveling 70 miles per hour downhill hoping to gain enough speed for the next mountain. It does not work. Downhill momentum is not sufficient for the long uphill grind. A person truly enjoys mountain biking when he or she can coast during times of downhill momentum and then gear down during the uphill climb.

You may notice your lack of patience or steadfastness when you pray for someone's need and you quickly give up when you see no quick change. Embrace the apparent setbacks. Never give up, no matter what happens or who rejects you. You have been accepted "into this grace—state of God's favor—in which we [firmly and safely] stand" (5.2b).

Endurance, in turn, produces character. The Weymouth translation of Romans 5.4a calls this "ripeness of character." There are people who work miracles but whose personal lives do not measure up to the ministry they profess. How does this happen? They bypass the tribulation in their lives that produces character. Instead of embracing trouble, they choose to avoid it. For example, instead of dealing with financial pressure, they continue to spend money on extravagant luxuries, instead of sowing seed money into others' needs. Or, to avoid family pressures, they choose a separation or a divorce rather than working through spousal problems in order to keep their vows and family together.

If you want Godly character, embrace God-ordained pressures —family pressure, financial pressure, spiritual pressure, academic pressure, ministry pressure, etc. God wants to take our thimble-size cups and stretch them to the size of vessels large enough to contain more and more of His glory. He has promised never to test you more than you are able to bear (see 1 Cor. 10.13 and 2 Cor. 4.17).

People mistakenly allow the trouble and tribulation in their lives to produce bitterness. For example, when someone does them wrong, they deposit the offenses in their "perfect" memory banks. They never seem to deal with offenses as they arise; instead, they wait for months or even years to bring them up, turning the once life-giving water into bitter poison. The good news is that when someone does you wrong (which happens again and again), you can let go of it. Place it in Jesus' hands instead of your memory bank, and it will not turn bitter or resentful inside you. We all need the healing touch of Jesus made available to us through the Cross. Without the Cross, our hurts turn into resentment and bitterness. Practice dealing with offenses quickly. Even in the natural a person would be considered negligent if he or she were injured and refused to go to a doctor. When pain continues, infections set in when we do not deal with the cause. When you allow bitterness into your reservoir, you defile not only yourself, but also others who touch you (see Heb.12.15).

BLESSINGS MAY CAUSE OUR FACES TO SHINE, BUT CHARACTER GIVES US STRENGTH TO STAND.

Use the grace of God to deal with the tribulation when the pressure comes. It will enlarge your capacity for the glory of God. You are able to successfully enter the process of hope in tribulation to perseverance to character and on to more hope. This is how you become truly mature!

Are you full of joy now? "Moreover—let us also be full of joy now! Let us exult *and* triumph in our troubles *and* rejoice in our sufferings, knowing that pressure *and* affliction *and* hardship produce patient *and* unswerving endurance" (5.3). We are not matured by our blessings; we are matured by hope through tribulation to patience, which produces ripeness of character. Blessings may cause our faces to shine, but character gives us strength to stand. Be joyful in this! You are now ready to start the process over again on even a higher level.

You now have access to God, but does God have access to you? Romans chapters 5 through 8 open our understanding to the way we experience the fullness of God's glory. He wants us to grow so that our joy is not dried up in a matter of days or even decades. He wants us to be men and women who faithfully walk with Him through trouble, tribulation, and hurt showing forth the glory of God. There are mature saints who have continually rejected bitterness and resentment. They remain unswerving in their faith. They are genuinely mature, sincerely joyous, and glorying in the hope of His eternal reward.

Chapter 16
JUSTIFIED

Now that we know we are declared righteous by grace through faith alone, not the Law, the Defense lays out the pathway for a righteous believer.

> While we were yet in weakness—powerless to help ourselves—at the fitting time Christ died for (on behalf of) the ungodly. Now it is an extraordinary thing for one to give his life even for an upright man, though perhaps for a noble *and* lovable *and* generous benefactor someone might even dare to die. But God shows *and* clearly proves His [own] love for us by the fact that while we were still sinners, Christ (the Messiah, the Anointed One) died for us. Therefore, since we are now justified—acquitted, made righteous, and brought into right relationship with God—by Christ's blood, how much more [certain is it that] we shall be saved by Him from the indignation and wrath of God. (Rom. 5.6-9)

The Biblical text states we are "now justified." Our justification is in the present tense. Someone might say, "You do not know my past life. Since I was saved, I have fallen." It is not simply your acknowledgement of sin that saves you; it is your confession of His completed work on Calvary that trumps your sin. To "confess" means, "to say the same thing." When you agree with God that "all have sinned and come short of the glory of God," His blood applies to you.

I was sitting in a Sunday school class with other young boys. My brother and I were fidgeting around with a mischievous gleam in our eyes when the teacher came into the class. She said, "Does God love good little boys?" We all answered, "Yeesss!" Then, looking directly at my brother and me, she asked, "Does God love bad little boys?" To which we all answered, "Noooo!" The truth of the matter is, God loves good boys and bad boys the same. His love is equal to them all. Her words to us that day influenced my negative thinking for many years. The truth is, Christ died for us while we were bad boys and bad girls.

All of mankind is under the weight of the Law and has been proven guilty before the just and holy Judge. Admitting we are sinners does not push us away from God; it brings us closer to Him. He knows we are formed from dust and in need of His forgiveness. Remember, when I was unsaved, one "good deed" did not save me. I may have donated to a charity or helped an old lady across the street. Whatever I did was not enough to save me. Since one good deed did not save me, then one bad deed does not "unsave" me when I am saved. Do not be harder on yourself than the Holy Spirit is. His conviction brings correction and cleansing if we yield to it, not condemnation.

The devil is a hard taskmaster; His condemnation brings depression and death. He beats and accuses you and even sends others to assist. When you look in a full-length mirror you see yourself and know there are certain blemishes. God does not use our blemishes against us. He gently performs surgery to remove the blemishes. In fact, God does not just do a little plastic surgery on us; He takes out our bent to sin. He is changing all of us who believe in His Son more and more into His divine image (2 Cor. 3.18). Romans says it all—we are justified. As a woman cannot be half pregnant, so a believer cannot be half justified.

You can take a pig out of a pigpen, but you cannot take the pigpen out of the pig. You can wash him, splash him with a lot of aftershave, and send him out for judging. You must keep a close watch on him until he makes it to the blue ribbon contest. After the contest, you are exhausted and when you look away for one second, your pig finds the nearest mud hole in which to waddle. That is because your pig still has a pig nature within. What God does for each of us personally in time is He removes our stubborn "pig" nature, otherwise known as our carnal sinful flesh.

Being fully justified does not mean we are fully aligned and in balance. We still become a little imbalanced after a lot of wear and tear. As a car needs alignments, so God keeps aligning us by the correction of His rod and staff. Before the alignment, the vehicle pulled toward the right or left side of the road. After the alignment, it drives straight, turning only at the touch of the driver. Our obedience of faith keeps us headed straight on into God's purposes, not swerving off course. As we keep following God's direction, we will continue to be changed from glory to glory (see 2 Cor. 3.18).

THE PRINCIPLE OF HIGHER KINGDOM DRAWS UP LOWER KINGDOM

A long time ago, in a faraway land, there was a little piece of mineral deep in the ground. The little mineral dreamed to himself, "Oh, if I could only be a piece of grass, lift my little head above this heavy soil, and begin to wave in the breeze, then I will be free!" One day the blades of grass in the kingdom of vegetation reached down into the mineral kingdom and brought the little mineral up to the surface.

The former mineral was now grass waving in the breeze as it stood with all the other blades of grass. He dreamed again, "I wish I could be like that cow over there, resting under a tree in the cool shade. It's sweltering here in the blazing sun. But I have a big problem. I have no legs to take me there."

Then the cow reached his mouth down to the lower kingdom of vegetation, ate, and digested that blade of grass. Just as the grass had wished, he was now lifted into a higher kingdom with legs to move about. Now he was part of the animal kingdom. When the upper kingdom reached down, the former mineral was lifted up and was no longer known by the name of the lower kingdom, but took his identity from the higher kingdom. No one pats a cow and says, "Good piece of grass." Everyone now says, "Good piece of beef."

The cow that was resting in the shade, now wandered around until she became so exhausted that she mused, "I wish I could ride around in an air-conditioned car like that man over there." One day, in the faraway land, the man walked over and killed the cow. He cooked the beef and ate it. No one ever thought to slap the man on his side and tease, "Now that's a nice side of beef." The cow was raised from her lower animal kingdom into the higher human kingdom, and now gained a new identity.

There are two lessons to learn when something moves from a lower kingdom into a higher one. *The first lesson is that the upper kingdom must first reach down into the lower kingdom. The second lesson is that the lower kingdom loses its lower kingdom identity and its former nature and takes on the nature and identity of the higher kingdom.* In this story the mineral became part of the vegetation after the blades of grass pulled it up, the grass became a part of the cow after the cow reached down, and the cow became a part of the man after the man reached down. These same two lessons may be observed in God's Kingdom. The Father sent His Son down to earth from His Heavenly Kingdom in order to lift mankind up to Himself. When anyone accepts His Son, he or she loses their former lower nature and identity and receives His instead.

The whole of creation groans for a manifestation of the sons of God (Rom. 8.22). You and I and all of nature groan within and cry out to God in our unredeemed state: "If only we could be like Jesus, the Son of God, we could walk through this life the way He walked." Can this happen? If so, how? The upper kingdom must reach down to the lower kingdom, which already happened two thousand years ago. God's dear Son Jesus Christ reached down into mankind's lowly kingdom. He came to lift us up into Himself. He took all of the mess, the vileness, and the chaos into Himself and made us brand new creatures in Christ Jesus. We are no longer known by our old, sinful, lower identities. We are known as children of God. There is no longer any need to belabor the fact that we were really, really bad sinners. I am now a new creature in Jesus Christ because, as the old hymn goes, "He reached down His hand for me." Thank God for Jesus!

WRATH AND JUDGMENT

We are free from wrath and judgment (5.9). The theme of chapter 5 is wrath versus justification. As a believer, I am free from the wrath of God and the penalty of sin. The devil has no legal right to demand payment for what I have done. My debt was paid in full at Calvary.

Be encouraged by the powerful truth in Romans 5.10, "For if while we were enemies we were reconciled to God through the death of His Son, it is much more [certain], now that we are reconciled, that we shall be saved [daily delivered from sin's dominion] through His [resurrection] life." This truth is dynamic! It has dynamic power to pull us out of the pits of depression. The focus is not on our past failures, but on His present keeping power day by day.

If Christ had the power to save you yesterday, does He not have that same power to keep you today? He saved you by His blood when you were His enemy. Just think about how closely He watches you now that you are His child and His friend! His power is infinite. His supernatural power is available to you and me to live abundant lives. Believe, confess, and live as a citizen of the Kingdom of God! In His Kingdom we may ". . . rejoice and exultingly glory in God [in His love and perfection] through our Lord Jesus Christ, through Whom we have now received and enjoy [our] reconciliation" (11).

"Your Honor," the Counsel continues, "I will take full responsibility for these freed sinners, now that they are justified." The One Righteous Man, Jesus, provides for all of us sinners. He represents us as we identify with Him.

have power by virtue of the fact of what Jesus Christ did. Jesus Christ represents all of us who are now in right relationship with Him. Christ —our Lawyer, our Advocate, our Savior—entered the courtroom, identified with us and set us free. This principle of identification "in Christ" makes His death our death and His victory our victory.

LINEAL HISTORY FROM ENTRANCE OF SIN TO EXTENT OF GRACE

The three main characters of Romans 5.12-21 are Adam, Moses, and Jesus Christ. Adam's disobedience ushered in the reign of sin that leads to death:

> Therefore, as sin came into the world through one man and death as the result of sin, so death spread to all men . . . because all men sinned. [To be sure,] sin was in the world before ever the Law was given, but sin is not charged to men's account where there is no law [to transgress]. Yet death held sway from Adam to Moses [the Lawgiver], even over those who did not themselves transgress [a positive command] as Adam did. Adam was a type (prefigure) of the One Who was to come [in reverse, the former destructive, the Latter saving]. (Rom. 5.12-14)

Moses followed and ushered in the reign of the Law, which, because of our weakness to obey it, also leads to death. Jesus Christ ushered in the reign of grace and righteousness, which leads to eternal life!

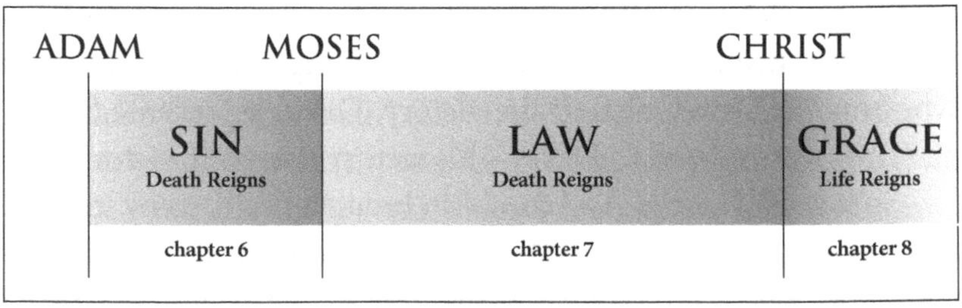

Three leaders. Three outcomes. Every human being descends from Adam; thus, we all inherit sin and its death through our humanity. We entered the reign of sin at conception. Most of humanity realizes the Law that came through Moses is good; however, there is one very big problem—no one is able to keep all of the Law. The flesh is not able to do what the Law requires: "What the Law could not do, [its power] being weakened by the flesh [that is, the entire nature of man without the Holy Spirit]" (Rom. 8.3a). The weakness of the Law is not in the Law itself, but rather in the flesh that futilely tries to keep it. Death is still the outcome even for those who try to live well but fail to keep the whole Law. Finally, at just the right time, Jesus Christ ushered in His reign of righteousness and grace that leads to life. God the Father's total plan of salvation is all wrapped up in the one God/Man Jesus Christ. All who submit to Jesus Christ's reign are in Him and enjoy His victory!

In other words, Jesus smote the giant, the devil, on the Cross, and we who are in Him inherit His victory for us. Jesus Christ cancelled what Adam did. It is not by choice that we are in Adam; it is by birth. However, it is by choice we are born again into Christ.

God's gift of salvation is disproportionate to our sin. Thank God for His limitless, immeasurable superabundant grace. It is so much greater it cannot be compared to sin:

> But God's free gift is not at all to be compared to the trespass—His grace is out of all proportion to the fall of man. For if many died through one man's falling away—his lapse, his offense—much more profusely did God's grace and the free gift [that comes] through the undeserved favor of the one Man Jesus Christ, abound and overflow to and for [the benefit of] many. Nor is the free gift at all to be compared to the effect of that one [man's] sin. (Rom. 5.15-16a)

Some of us may be like the little fish swimming around in the ocean worrying what will happen when we drink the ocean dry. We see ourselves as little guppies in an ocean of God's grace, and we worry about running out of water. Stop worrying. You and I can no more exhaust the grace of God than a guppy can drink the ocean dry. Even all of the whales in existence have not been able to drink any ocean dry!

YOU AND I CAN NO MORE EXHAUST THE GRACE OF GOD THAN A GUPPY CAN DRINK THE OCEAN DRY.

Others of us are more like little birds preparing to leave the nest. "What if I fly so far that I run out of air?" we obsessively worry. This kind of bird likes to gather at conferences to discuss the consequences of running out of airspace. These birds never learn the answers to their questions because they "safely" sit on a limb to conserve what little airspace surrounds them. You and I can no more exhaust the grace of God than a sparrow can fly beyond the boundaries and limits of the sky above. Awesome grace!

Chapter 17

REIGNING IN CHRIST

125

In Christ we are kings. Romans 5.17 clearly states this fact: "For if, because of one man's trespass (lapse, offense) death reigned through that one, much more surely will those who receive [God's] overflowing grace (unmerited favor) and the free gift of righteousness . . . reign as kings in life through the One, Jesus Christ, the Messiah, the Anointed One." Presently we have the privilege of reigning with God in Christ. Sometimes it surely does not look to us as though we are reigning royalty. When we see our circumstances only through earthly eyes, we still see the negative, but from a heavenly perspective, it looks positively different.

Our heavenly seating arrangements are described in Ephesians 1.20 and 2.6: "Which He exerted in Christ when He raised Him from the dead and seated Him at His [own] right hand in the heavenly [places] . . . And He raised us up together with Him and made us sit down together—giving us joint seating with Him—in the heavenly sphere [by virtue of our being] in Christ Jesus, the Messiah, the Anointed One." When we shift our focus to the heavenly sphere, we see a much bigger picture. We are able to see Christ's victory from His first coming to His second coming. All of the problems in between are minor "speed bumps" in life's journey. The higher kingdom has lifted us up. We have a new royal identity and a new perspective and purpose for life.

What David did to the Philistine, Jesus Christ did to our enemy, the devil. Our enemy taunts us to argue and fight. We need to stand and speak forth the truth that will set us free. In Jesus Christ alone is the victory that already defeated the devil, by making an open spectacle of him (Col. 2.13-15).

each of them separately: "How close can you drive to the edge of a cliff on a mountain road?" The first responder said, "I can come within two feet of the edge." The second said, "I have much experience; I can come within one foot of the edge." The executive hired the third man to be his chauffeur because he said, "I will stay as far away as possible!" Do not walk so close to the edge of the permissible less you be seduced by the forbidden.

THEORIES ON THE NATURE OF SIN

There is an erroneous doctrine which teaches that once a person is born again, sin no longer exists in the saved person. This is called the doctrine of eradication. This doctrine teaches that the old nature is totally eradicated by a definite second work of grace. In some of John Wesley's early Methodist doctrine we may read about this second definite work of grace. In other words, at a separate second encounter with God after salvation, sin completely dies to a person. It is a weak argument in light of reality. Have you looked around at your saved brothers and sisters? Have you found one who is without sin? If you think you have, stick around; your delusion will soon be cleared up.

THE OLD LIFE IS IMPOSSIBLE!

Now, in chapter 6, verses 1 and 15 the apostle Paul asks the same basic question: Should we who believe continue to sin so that grace may abound? He answers both times with an emphatic, "Certainly not!" Never! Then he poses another question to remind his readers of the facts they already know: We have been set free from sin, so how could we possibly continue sinning? In other words, are we to remain under the power of sin? Or shall we move on to something new and dynamic? Of course, we must move on. The old life is impossible!

If we were to take home a fish out of an ice-covered pond and put it under the bed covers to warm up, it would die. By the same token, if on a hot summer day we took a big, fluffy cat and held it under cool pond water, it would die. Why? The fish and the cat would be violating their basic natures. A fish was not made to live on land and a cat was not made to live under water. When we believers stumble back into our old ways, we are stepping with our new natures into old ruts of pre-salvation behavior. We are not born again to live our new lives in our old nature habitat. Living out the old life is impossible in Jesus Christ. In Him everything is being made new. ". . . Old things are passed away; behold, all things are become new" (*KJV*, 2 Cor. 5.17).

HE HAS ADEQUATE GRACE

Because of the Cross, sin is no problem for God. He wants us to know when we have sinned; He has adequate grace to wash away all of our sin. His grace is greater than the oceans. You and I may take all of the grace of God we need, no matter how many times we need it. "If we confess our sins, he is faithful and just and will forgive . . ." (*NIV*, 1 Jn. 1.9). When we go to God humbly and repentant, He ministers His grace and forgiveness. He will never turn us away because of His lack of sufficient grace. "Are you ignorant of the fact that all of us who have been baptized into Christ Jesus were baptized into His death? We were buried therefore with Him by the baptism into death, so that just as Christ was raised from the dead by the glorious [power] of the Father, so we too might habitually live and behave in newness of life. For if we have become one with Him by sharing a death like His, we shall also be [one with Him in sharing] His resurrection [by a new life lived for God]" (Rom. 6.3-5).

BAPTIZED INTO NEW LEADERSHIP

This book is not an exegesis on the whole concept of baptism, but to make the study of the book of Romans complete, the subject of baptism cannot be ignored. The standard description of baptism is "an outward sign of an inward work." One aspect of the inward change baptism signifies is the transition to new leadership.

In the tenth chapter of 1 Corinthians there is a good reference to the new leadership baptism brings. This chapter retells the Old Testament story of the children of Israel who, after serving Pharaoh for 400 years, traveled through the Red Sea on their way out of Egypt. Passing through the Red Sea represented their "baptism" unto Moses and it publicly declared their desire to follow Moses' leadership instead of Pharaoh's. After Moses died, Joshua took over leadership. What did the Israelites do to declare their acceptance of his leadership? They went through the Jordan River as a "baptism" of accepting Joshua as their new commander.

In the early New Testament church, some still held onto Judaism. When these people were saved, they were baptized with the baptism of John the Baptist in the wilderness. They acknowledged John the Baptist as their new spiritual leader. This is why John stated when he baptized Jesus in the Jordan River, "Behold the Lamb of God, which taketh away the sin of he world" (*KJV*, Jn. 1.29). In this statement, John was redirecting his followers' allegiance from himself to Jesus. This was not easy for many of them to do. In fact, they went to John in prison to ask if Jesus was really the One for whom they had been waiting. John affirmed to them—Jesus was the Messiah.

BAPTIZED SELF IS ALREADY DEAD

Baptism applies only to a "dead" person. It is the sign of burial. If someone were in your house taking final gasps of breath, no one would go outside to begin digging a grave. This would be most inappropriate! The burial process is not begun until after a person is pronounced dead. Similarly, baptism is performed after a person has identified himself or herself with Christ in His death and His subsequent resurrection. Baptism is an outward sign of death and resurrection with Christ. As He was buried, so is a believer buried in the water. As He rose from the dead, so a believer rises from the water to newness of life. Only in Jesus Christ is a believer now able to live in victory and newness of life (Jn. 11.25-26).

Someone may argue, "But the devil knocks me down when I am weak and so I sin." Confess aloud what you believe in your heart, "The devil has been defeated. This is fact and has nothing to do with my feelings. Jesus beat my enemy. The giant is dead!" Your feelings do not intimidate your enemy. The truth causes the enemy to flee. Hallelujah! He must go. You are free indeed!

It seems so primitive; it seems so simple. Someone takes a person by the hand and baptizes him or her. Why do we have to do this? We are baptized because He asked us to do it. We follow Him into the waters of baptism as an act of obedience and an outward confession of what has already taken place inside—we who believe have died to our old natures. We confess through baptism that we accept the new leadership of the One who took our sin. He is our new leader. He is the author and the finisher of our salvation.

ACCEPTING NEW LEADERSHIP

When the Israelites accepted Moses' and then Joshua's new leadership, it was through public baptism. Subsequently, they went forth and conquered under their new leader. Before we were saved, there were two bosses running our lives: Satan and self. One demanded, "Do this!" and the other ordered, "Do that!" They were never satisfied. We were under their constant scrutiny and condemnation. One was always in the courtroom bringing more accusations before the Judge.

Now, however, we are born again. Satan has been defeated, and in Christ we are dead to sin. Satan knows this truth, but self sticks around. Self is now our major problem. Many people are baptized; yet they do not turn their lives over to the new leadership of Christ. They prefer self-leadership. They take only part of the full salvation package, the part that covers their sins by the blood of Christ and accepts them into heaven. They fail to submit to the total leadership of the Commander-in-Chief Jesus Christ. This sets up an ongoing struggle between submitting to the leadership of self and the leadership of Christ. The blood of Christ washes away and forgives the sin, but the Cross of Christ deals with self—the greater the acceptance, the less the struggle.

Impossible! Impossible! The ongoing old life is impossible under His new leadership. How can we possibly go on sinning? He is leading us away from sin not into it. When we see ourselves sinning, we should know that self is leading at that point instead of Christ. Self has no right to lead. When we were baptized, we publicly declared our allegiance to our new leader Jesus Christ. The loving One, my Savior and Lord, who died for me is the leader of my life. I love Him more than my old appetites for sin. Praise the Lord!

THE OLD SERVICE IS IMPOSSIBLE!

If you take verse 16 out of its chapter 6 setting and allow the enemy to isolate it, you may put yourself back under his condemnation. "Do you not know that if you continually surrender yourself to any one to do his will, you are the slave of him whom you obey . . . ." This verse teaches that as you are taking orders, the one you habitually obey is your boss. Think about this. Apply it to yourself. Who have I been habitually obeying in the last few days? When I honestly evaluate my days, I may come up with the condemning truth. How many times did I allow my flesh to lead me into overeating, anger toward someone, being ungrateful, boasting about myself, gossiping, disobeying the Spirit's voice, and on and on the list could go? You will recognize your fleshly leadership when you allow the Holy Spirit to convict you, so don't condemn yourself. Tempted to evaluate others instead of your self? The flesh is again in charge. When I am not under the leadership of Christ, I am yielding to my flesh's leadership and here the devil has room to insert questionable temptations.

Now, place verse 16 back into its setting and read it connected to verse 17 for the rest of the story:

> Do you not know that if you continually surrender yourselves to any one to do his will, you are the slaves of him whom you obey, whether that be to sin, which leads to death, or to obedience which leads to righteousness . . . . But thank God, though you were once slaves of sin you have become obedient with all your heart to the standard of teaching in which you were instructed *and* to which you were committed.

The old service is impossible! You and I are no longer slaves of the devil. "But you've sinned three times already today!" the devil accuses me. My quick reply is, "That does not mean I am your slave. I thank God through Jesus Christ, who saved me and imparted His life into me, that I accept His good and divine leadership which was declared at my baptism." Each day God's new straight path takes me further away from the old roots and right to His heart.

When the devil highlights verse 16, we who believe must highlight verse 17. When you dwell on evil thoughts, realize that you have subjected yourself to the leadership of Satan or self. Satan will try to use that failure to trick you back into thinking he is your boss. He is not. Jesus Christ is your boss. Even though you fail and sin, it is only part of the story. The rest of the story is that "If we [freely] admit that we have sinned *and* confess our sins, He is faithful and just . . . and will forgive our sins . . ." (1 Jn. 1.9). We should be extremely thankful about this gracious plan!

Verse 17 begins by reminding us of our true leader: "But thank God" (AB), "But God be thanked" (*KJV*), and "But thanks be to God" (*NIV*). If we believe in verse 17 as well as verse 16, we are able to take a very positive redeeming approach to our failures. Start spending more time thanking God for his goodness, and less time groveling over your past failures which have been confessed and forgiven. Amen!

The old service is impossible! We get tired serving because we try so hard. Stop trying and start yielding. Yield to the Spirit of Christ, and He will lead you through His death and into His life and power! Why do we put ourselves down when we fail? This does not make matters better; in fact, it makes things worse. Our failures are no match to the tremendous price paid for us. Our salvation with its accompanying justification and sanctification are not a result of our promise to God, but are the result of God's promise to us! He always keeps His promises. It is not feeling good that makes you free. You are free because of God's divine decree. You are not free by what you did yesterday. You are free because of what Jesus did for you two thousand years ago on the Cross!

YOU ARE FREE BECAUSE OF WHAT JESUS DID FOR YOU TWO THOUSAND YEARS AGO ON THE CROSS!

When justice demands that you be judged for your sin, you must focus on the One who stepped into the courtroom at just the right moment with nail-scarred hands and said, "I paid it *all.*" Focus on the victory of the One whose victory is greater than David's, whose riches are greater than Solomon's, and whose leadership is greater than Moses'. Focus on Jesus Christ.

When you are under a cloud of condemnation because of your failures, remember Paul's quote of Psalm 32.1-2, "Blessed are they whose transgressions are forgiven, whose sins are covered. Blessed is the man whose sin the Lord will never count against him" (*NIV*, Rom. 4.7-8). It is reported that St. Augustine had this Scripture at the foot of his dying bed. Meditate, also, on Romans 5.17 and 6.17, ". . . much more surely will those who receive [God's] overflowing grace (unmerited favor) and the free gift of righteousness . . . reign as kings in life through the one Man Jesus Christ (the Messiah, the Anointed One)" and "But thank God, though you were once slaves of sin, you have become obedient with all your heart to the standard of teaching in which you were instructed and to which you were committed." We are free by His divine decree!

Blessed are they whose transgressions are forgiven, whose sins are covered.

In the beginning of Romans chapter 6 Paul asked, "Shall we go on sinning so that grace may increase?" (*NIV*). He asked this question because it could be a logical deduction after spending two chapters explaining how free believers are. "God forbid" (*KJV*) was his emphatic answer. Man's natural reasoning alone would result in the wrong conclusion, so Paul answers with his strongest statement yet: "Not at all." "Let it never be so." How can we who are dead to sin, possibly live a life of sin? Never. Don't you as a believing reader already know the old service is impossible? The old deeds have no place in your life because they are powerless. You have a new nature; you are a new creature with a divine purpose.

Recall the story of the cat and the fish earlier in this chapter. If the cat is thrown into the lake or, for that matter, falls out of the boat, its real nature cries out to get back into the boat. If, for whatever reason, you fall "out of the boat" of fellowship, your new nature in Christ will cry out even as Peter, "Lord, save me" (*KJV*, Matt. 14.30b). Likewise, Jesus will lift you out of the waves and back into the boat. Your new nature does not pine for the old environment. The further we get down the road from the old haunts, the less influence they have over us. The further an astronaut travels from earth, the less the power of gravity holds him down.

Chapter 19
UNION WITH GOD

In the first part of Romans chapter 6 we learned that believers identify themselves with Christ's death through baptism, as they make a public declaration of His life, death, and resurrection. The remainder of chapter 6 explains the believer's relationship to sin and the keys to freedom from its dominion. Every believer has two basic problems: one problem is with sin and the other is with the Law. Chapter 7 of Romans covers the believer's relationship to the Law.

Three words, used in the *King James Version*, establish the process of sanctification in chapter 6. The first word is "know" (6.6), the second word is "reckon" (11), and the third word is "yield" (13).

KNOW

Go ahead and read the whole of chapter 6 in your Bible in order to get a broader understanding of the word *know*. Then return to verses 12 and 13 that say, "Let not sin therefore rule as king in your mortal (short-lived, perishable) bodies, to make you yield to their cravings and be subject to their lusts *and* evil passions. Do not continue offering or yielding your bodily members [and faculties] to sin as instruments (tools) of wickedness. But offer *and* yield yourselves to God as though you have been raised from the dead to [perpetual] life, and your bodily members [and faculties] to God, presenting them as implements of righteousness." Do the cravings, the lusts, and the evil passions of verse 12 remind you of chapter 5 and verse 20: "The law was added so that the trespass might increase . . ."? If you read only part of the Word of God, the devil can use that partial Word to bring greater condemnation to your life. The devil has a PhD in accusing and deceiving the saints.

When I finish reading verses 12 and 13, I may feel a little heavy in my spirit. Do I still have the potential for sin to rule in my life? Knowing how weak we humans are, why are we reminded of our weakness right in the middle of the "freedom" chapters? Our weakness is an important part of the whole truth. The whole truth follows in verse 14, "For sin shall not [any longer] exert dominion over you, since now you are not under Law [as slaves], but under grace [as subjects of God's favor and mercy]."

THE HEAVINESS OF THE LAW HAS BEEN TURNED INTO THE FREEDOM OF A PROMISE.

You must understand that your body is an instrument free to serve God. Your attention is not on rules such as, "Do not do this" and "Don't you dare break that Law." Your attention has been freed to submit to God because verse 14 tells us we are not going to sin if we continue to offer or yield our bodily members as instruments to God. It is His promise to us. The heaviness of the Law has been turned into the freedom of a promise. Continue to focus on His promise —His covenant—and not on failures, for, "He Who began a good work in you, will continue until the day of Jesus Christ" (Phil. 1.6a).

One day a baby eagle was put into a barnyard with chickens. The eagle was tethered so it could not fly away. As the eagle grew, it scratched and pecked the ground and acted just like the chickens around it. One day, after the eagle had grown to its full size, a man stopped by the farm and thought it a pity to tether such a magnificent bird to the ground. So, he paid the farmer for the eagle and cut the tether to set it free. The eagle, however, stayed in the barnyard and continued to scratch the ground and peck for corn. No matter how hard the man tried to get the eagle to fly, it refused. Finally, in frustration, the man took the great bird up into the mountains where there were other eagles. Once there, he set it free—free to be what it was created to be. Its giant wings caught the warm currents and lifted the great bird to the clouds. The man had to take the eagle away from the chickens in the barnyard to get it to soar like the eagle it really was. So it is with you and me. If you believe what God says about you, your outlook will change and step-by-step you will rise up with wings as the eagle you were meant to be.

Have you ever met good saints who were under a cloud of depression? Perhaps Satan obsessively repeats Romans 6.16 only into their inner ears, "Do you not know that if you continually surrender yourselves to anyone to do his will, you are the slaves of him whom you obey?" Our enemy uses this portion of Scripture many times to cause good saints to feel depressed. These poor saints are being beaten up by a part of Scripture that is really a negative question used to invoke God's positive answer. The positive answer comes in verse 17, "But thank God, though you were once slaves of sin, you have become obedient with all your heart to the standard of teaching in which you were instructed and to which you were committed." Verse 16 is not meant to trigger depression, rather it is meant to trigger our praise for God's abundant provision.

Do not let sin have dominion over you! It has no power over the believer who walks in newness of life. The verse that frees the believer to live victoriously is verse 14: "For sin shall not [any longer] exert dominion over you . . ." Through the inspiration of the Holy Spirit, the apostle Paul asks thoughtful questions, not to trip up his audience, but rather to enlighten his readers to one very clear answer—we believers have true freedom in Christ.

While enjoying a picnic in the Nairobi game park, my wife and I, along with our two children and another missionary, sat in a picnic area at what we thought was a safe distance from the animals. Although most of the animals were at a distance, the baboons and monkeys were in the nearby trees. Suddenly, I turned to see a big baboon carrying away my four-year-old daughter. Instantly we realized what he really wanted was the banana she was holding.

"Throw the banana down!" we yelled. When she did, the baboon put her down and ran up the tree with his favorite bright yellow fruit. Similarly, the devil tries to take advantage of us when we reach into his territory and hang on to what he thinks is his. Throw it down and walk away free from his clutches. He only comes to kill and steal.

I choose to live in the glorious light revealed in verses 17 and 18: "But thank God, though you were once slaves of sin, you have become obedient with all your heart . . . And, having been set free from sin, you have become the servants of righteousness . . . ." This confession is beneficial to all the saints for we are free to be servants of righteousness! His Word is greater than your feelings or the enemy's accusations.

Paul wants to make sure that you truly understand what he is teaching when he explains in verse 19: "I am speaking in familiar human terms, because of your natural limitations. For as you yielded your bodily members [and faculties] as servants to impurity and ever increasing lawlessness, so now yield your bodily members [and faculties] once for all as servants to righteousness—right being and doing—[which leads] to sanctification." It cannot be said any clearer.

YOU AND I MAY STILL HAVE PROBLEMS AND STRUGGLES; HOWEVER, WHEN WE BELIEVE WHAT THE WORD OF GOD DECLARES ABOUT US WE EMBRACE WHAT JESUS DIED TO MAKE US—FREE!

Then Paul goes on to explain the prior "benefit" package people received when yielding to sin, impurity, and lawlessness. The first "benefit" was they were free from righteousness: "For when you were slaves of sin, you were free in regard to righteousness" (6.20). The last "benefit" was the "death benefit:" "But then what benefit (return) did you get from the things of which you are now ashamed? [None,] for the end of those things is death" (21).

We do not need to wallow in our past because ". . . you have been set free from sin and have become the slaves of God, you have your present reward in holiness and its end is eternal life" (22). Wow! I love this verse. As believers our present benefit package includes holiness and eternal life. How is that for a great anti-depressant? You and I may still have problems and struggles; however, when we believe what the Word of God declares about us, we embrace what Jesus died to make us—free!

Sin pays death: "For the wages which sin pays is death . . ." Some Christians may only know this first half of verse 23. If you are one who lives in condemnation, read the whole verse: " . . . but the [bountiful] free gift of God is eternal life through (in union with) Jesus Christ." Are you receiving the deadly wages you have worked for or are you receiving the free gift of life you haven't worked for?

RECKON

Taken from the accounting field, *to reckon* means, "to put to the account of." When a person "reckons" something, it means he or she is banking on the fact that money was put to the person's account.

We who believe are banking on the fact that as David killed Goliath, all of the Israelites who were in David received the rewards of his victory. David's victory was put to the account of all of the Israelites, and they were no longer under the domination of the Philistines. Furthermore, believers bank on the fact that when Jesus Christ died and was resurrected, His victory was credited to our account. Watchman Nee said, "Our old history ends with the Cross; our new history begins with the Resurrection." Our old nature was crucified with Christ. Just as His death is your death, so His resurrection is your resurrection. His victory is your victory. His life is your life!

YIELD

Romans 6.13 commands us to yield our members to God as instruments of righteousness. Herein lies the secret of walking in ongoing victory. When you are tempted to sin, there is something you can do—yield to God instead of the sin. Confess aloud: "Lord, I offer my bodily members to you!" Then listen for His voice to direct your mind, your hands, your mouth, your tongue, your feet, etc. His voice will align you with His written Word. Finally, you must obey His direction in order to become an instrument of righteousness. Yielding to God is the product of a life that knows, reckons, and trusts Him who is trustworthy. To whom do you practice yielding? God? Sinful desires? Self?

We are made to reign. If we do not reign over sin, it will reign over us. As a teenager driving in upstate New York in the fall, my friends and I had the opportunity to buy three gallons of fresh apple cider in one-gallon glass jugs. I hate to say it, but we planned to let them ferment into hard cider. We placed the jugs in the back seat before driving into a fog and spinning around in the dark of the night. The three jugs smashed into each other, soaking the rear seat and floor with cider. We cleaned up most of the mess, but for many months the remaining cider fermented and the smell reminded us of our ill intentions. Likewise, when we are born again, odors of our past life involvement may linger.

We have already established the fact that when Christ died, we died with Him. Through Christ we have the right and the power to reign over our mortal bodies. There may still be some "cider" smell, but we are clean and walk in the light. The world and the enemy will tell us there is no power in the Gospel. Do not believe the lies. Do not be talked out of the truth! The Gospel is the power of God!

WE ARE MADE TO REIGN. IF WE DO NOT REIGN OVER SIN, IT WILL REIGN OVER US.

It may be true that you have some old habits hanging on to you. Your bad habit is like a dead leaf hanging on to a healthy tree. When autumn comes, all of the leaves die and most fall to the ground, however, a few continue to hang on to the tree. You may spend all winter throwing rocks at one dead, little leaf that still hangs on. You may even recruit others to throw rocks with you in an attempt to dislodge the withered-up leaf. You end up bruised and cut up from all of your attempts to remove one old dead leaf. On the other hand, you could just relax and wait for spring when the new life will surge up and the sap will push off every last, little, dried-up, withered-up leaf that has clung from last year. Life always conquers death.

Face it. Everyone has a few dead leaves here and there in this life that they would like to whack off. Are we going to spend our whole lives attempting to whack off a few persistent dried up leaves? Or, are we going to live and function in God and allow the new, redemptive, victorious, and wonderful life of Jesus to surge through us? As Christ's life works its way up through the roots, the trunk, and the branches of our lives, it carries life-giving sap to our limbs. Soon, the dead little leaf that was hanging on (which seemed like such a BIG problem) is gone. It has been driven off, not by our sticks and rocks, but by His new, inner current of divine life. The healthy tree yields itself fully to the rich sap. Miraculous results follow. Know it, reckon it, and yield to it!

I remember as a young boy trying to run up an escalator that was going down. The moment I stopped running, I was carried downward. Some Christians see their lives in the same way. But the truth of the matter is since we are "in Christ" we are on an escalator going up—standing still does not cause us to go down. Relax and enjoy the ride He has purchased for you. Stop trying and start trusting.

THE OLD UNION IS IMPOSSIBLE!

Again Paul questions a third time (see also 6.3 and16): "Do you not know, brethren, for I am speaking to men who are acquainted with the Law, that legal claims have power over a person only for so long as he is alive?" (Rom. 7.1). We are no longer subject to the Law once we have died. For example, is it legal to stop a speeding hearse and give a speeding ticket to the man in the coffin? Of course not! The man in the coffin died, so the law no longer applies to him. Since we have died with Christ, the old union is impossible!

Not only is the old life impossible and the old service impossible, but the old union is also just as impossible. Before we were saved, we were born in sin and married to the Law. Romans chapter 7 explains the believer's relationship to the Law. Paul begins by stating that marriage vows are binding until one of the married partners dies: ". . . legal claims have power over a person only for as long as he is alive . . . but if her husband [a person] dies she is loosed and discharged from the law . . ." (1-2). Similarly, the binding union between the believer and the Law is broken because death has severed the relationship. Who died? Did the Law die? No. I died with Christ. And when He died I died, and was released from the Law, free to marry a new Partner. The Law does not apply to dead people!

Not only are we set free in Christ from sin and its power (chapter 6), but we are also set free from the Law and its condemnation (chapter 7). All of us would agree that sin is bad for us. Sin is certainly bad from God's point of view. But do we really need to be set free from the Law? After all, the Law is good; the Law is from God—the Law is eternal. Paul uses the marriage relationship in chapter 7 verses 1 through 4 to illustrate the answer to this question concerning the Law, "But if her husband dies, the marriage law no longer is binding on her—she is free from that law—and if she unites herself to another man she is not an adulteress" (7.3b).

Our difficulty is not with the Law itself. The Law is good, holy, and an expression of the divine attributes of God. Our problem is with our absolute inability to obey the Law to its fullest. How then do we break our relationship to sin? We die to it. How do we break our relationship to the Law? In the same way—we die to it. Christ's death includes both.

In the next chapter we will look carefully at the analogy used in verses 1 through 4. The husband is the Law and the believer is the wife. Before you were saved, you were married to the Law with all of its rules and regulations. Now you are legally free from the Law because one marriage partner died—YOU!

Chapter 20 COURTROOM: LEGALLY FREE FROM THE LAW

Slowly, a spirit of revelation dawns over you. It brings real conviction from the Holy Spirit, Who convicts you of your sin. Each defendant cries out in front of the witnesses, "Yes, **Your Honor,** You know and I know that I am sinner. I am guilty. Please forgive me of my sins."

"Your Honor, as a believer she is free from the Law," declares Jesus Christ our Defense.

"What do you mean, 'she is free from the Law'?" our accuser attacks.

"What I mean is she died with Christ, the One who walked into this courtroom with the visible evidence of nail-scarred hands! She is no longer legally bound to the Law. When she accepted Christ as her Savior, she died with Him and was born again by the One who breathed resurrection life into her."

Each defendant who trusts Christ now knows: "I have been crucified with Christ—[in Him] I have shared His crucifixion; it is no longer I who live, but Christ, the Messiah, lives in me; and the life I now live in the body I live by faith—by adherence to *and* reliance on and [complete] trust—in the Son of God, Who loved me and gave Himself up for me" (Gal. 2.20).

Once you accept the fact you died with Christ, you can start enjoying eternal life, free from the Law, which held you bound. You are now **legally free** to marry another. In this spiritual allegory you were a sleeping beauty who was kissed by the Prince who died for you.

NO LONGER MARRIED TO THE LAW

In this analogy, you and I are referred to as Mrs. Law, married to Mr. Law—each of us was legally joined to Mr. Law. God saw our sorry state and desired to set us free. Meanwhile, we had been scheming the demise of this impossible husband dictator, Mr. Law. "If I can't kill Mr. Law, maybe God will," I selfishly thought. "If I were free from Mr. Law, I could be such a happy person! Mr. Law is ruining my life. I have no freedom. He is so demanding and condemning, I can't take it any more!" My friends advised, "Just divorce him. You are better off without him." Then I remembered Romans 7.3, which I had memorized, "Accordingly, she will be held an adulteress if she unites herself to another man while her husband lives . . . ." Jesus' own words flooded my conscience, "And if she divorces her husband and marries another man, she commits adultery" (*NIV*, Mk. 10.12). "How can I possibly be freed from this condemnation and bondage?" I screamed in my inner being. Mr. Law haunted me. I tried to ignore him and pretend he didn't exist. Nothing worked. I was joined "'til death do us part."

"Likewise, my brethren, you have undergone death as to the Law through the [crucified] body of Christ, so that now you may belong to Another, to Him Who was raised from the dead in order that we may bear fruit for God" (Rom. 7.4). As I was so intent on getting rid of Mr. Law, God was concentrating on getting rid of me! Mr. Law did not need to die; I needed to die. God is not afraid of the death of His loved ones because He knows the power of resurrection. Jesus Christ is the only One who may be trusted with that much authority! The apostle Paul considered this point important for he repeats it to the Colossians, "For you died, and your life is now hidden with Christ in God" (*NIV*, 3.3).

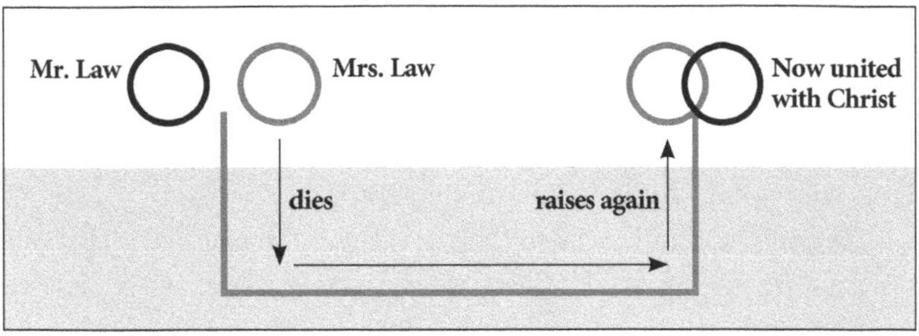

We also need several reminders that we are dead to the Law for we tend to imagine seeing Mr. Law spying on us to accuse us. "Aha!" You jump, as you pull your foot back from the street after ignoring the flashing "Do not walk!" sign. You can be sure Mr. Law was the one to shout when he saw you taking the slightest misstep. You continue to nervously keep vigil, trying not to break any of the rules he held you to for so long.

As far as legal ties go, once dead, you are free to be married to another. You have been legally freed to "marry" Jesus Christ, who alone is able to fulfill all of Mr. Law's requirements. Mr. Law could very well be keeping an eye on you. You do not suffer amnesia, forgetting everything of your former marriage to him. You remember all of your failures. You recall how everything Mr. Law said was true and right, and everything you did fell short. You think about how you always had to ask, "May I do this?" or "Is it OK to do that?" The feelings of nervousness return with intensity. Even though you are legally married to Another, you are still tempted to futilely defend yourself to Mr. Law.

In our old life Mr. Law stood over us, demanding that his coffee was brewed at just the right minute, temperature, and strength. In our new marriage to Jesus, it is very different. Jesus reaches out with His loving arms and assures us, "Don't worry about a thing. In fact, I have already put the coffee on for you, and it's just the way you like it. I have even prepared a few fish and loaves for you on the beach." This new covenant life will take some time for the wife to get used to, but it will happen as you respond to the embrace of your new Husband. Why not allow Jesus to defend you? Nothing can separate what God joins together, not even Mr. Law. Choose now to walk through life hand-in-hand with your new lover husband Jesus Christ. Enjoy your new marriage. He will empower you to fulfill your true destiny.

Before you and I came to Christ, we were mastered by sin. We are now free from sin in Christ. Thanks be to God, sin is not the controlling problem any more! Before you and I came to Christ, we were married to the Law. We are now free from the Law in Christ. Our kind Savior now directs our lives. He is a delight to be around. He is not looking for our missteps to beat us over the head. He is loving and thoughtful, full of mercy and grace.

**THANKS BE TO GOD,
SIN IS NOT THE PROBLEM ANY MORE!**

EXPERIENCING MARRIAGE WITH OUR NEW HUSBAND

If you are not feeling the victory, you may still be living as though you are married to Mr. Law. Stop entertaining him. You are married to another! Your current husband, Jesus Christ, is not abusive. Neither is he legalistic or irrational like your former husband. He is full of love and compassion toward you (see Exodus 34.6-7).

When the former Mrs. Law is joined to her new husband, Jesus Christ, at first she still gets nervous and upset when she makes a mess of something. Perhaps one day the former Mrs. Law begins to hysterically cry when she has an accident with the family car. She knows that Mr. Law would have scolded her severely before family and friends. How could she be so careless? Now her new husband sees the damage, and says, "What's the problem? I have already purchased insurance, and you will have a new car delivered shortly." This kind of reaction is so different from her former husband's who was so rigid and inflexible. Our new husband, Jesus, wants to lavish good gifts on us, yet we refuse them. We continue to live in bondage to Mr. Law, forgetting we have died to him and are made legally free.

In chapter 7 of Romans the word *Law* is used twenty-three times and the word I is used approximately thirty times. Chapter 7 is full of the Law and I. The Law and I had a hard- to-forget relationship for many years. Cannot there be a once-and-for-all act that frees me from the Law? There is. It is His death and burial. It has already taken place and needs to be refreshed in my thinking every day. It is the death of me. The apostle Paul recorded his daily death elsewhere when he penned the words, "I die daily—that is, that I face death every day and die to self" (1 Cor. 15.31b). I died, I am dying, and I will die, and I live in an ongoing relationship to another—Jesus Christ—Who gives me His life.

Mr. Law is probably the greatest culprit to quench Spirit-filled living. Mr. Law says, "You know, you should have gone to church last Sunday. You forsook the gathering together of the saints." If you are honest, you agree that you should have gone to church last Sunday. Once again, everything that Mr. Law says is true. This is why it is much more difficult for a believer to deal with the Law than with sin. Sin is wrong. The Law is holy.

So, how do we effectively deal with the Law? Through our relationship with our new husband, we deal with the Law. Picture this: you get up one morning and start to race through your day. Mr. Law shows up at your window with a huge placard asking, "Have you read your Bible today?" "No, I haven't read my Bible today!" you sarcastically yell back. Now you feel condemned. Not only did you not have time to read your Bible, but you also decided that you did have time to lose your temper.

"Perhaps something really bad will happen today as a result of your bad behavior," Mr. Law accuses. So, down on your knees, you plead, "Oh, God. Please forgive me. I swear I'll never do it again." Be careful not to make rash vows you cannot keep. Instead, always depend on His grace.

Just then, your new husband walks into the room and you quickly confess, "Honey, I didn't read my Bible today, and then I was frustrated with someone."

"It's all right," He confidently replies. "We will read the Bible together, and I will help you to not lose your temper in frustration." You can hardly believe His reaction is true. There is not another person like Him. He is full of grace, mercy, gentleness, goodness, longsuffering, and self-control. He knows who you really are and He still loves you without reservation. His mood is always good and his desire is to glorify His Father through you.

Stop! Ask the Holy Spirit to show you clearly the truth of how you have been delivered from your old husband, Mr. Law, by Christ's death. Allow Him to reign in your life. Live only for your loving Heavenly husband, Jesus Christ. Be free eternally!

THE LAW CAUSED SIN TO ABOUND

It is very important for us to understand:

> When we were living in the flesh (mere physical lives), the sinful passions that were awakened *and* aroused up by [what] the Law [makes sin] were constantly operating in our natural powers—in our bodily organs, in the sensitive appetites and wills of the flesh—so that we bore fruit for death. But now we are discharged from the Law *and* have terminated all intercourse with it, having died to what once restrained *and* held us captive. So now we serve not under [obedience to] the old code of written regulations, but [under obedience to the promptings] of the Spirit in newness [of life]. (Rom. 7.5-6)

Once again, the apostle reminds you of the terms of the new marriage, specifically the intimate intercourse of marriage. There is to be no more intercourse between the Law and the believer because one partner (the believer) has died.

"What then do we conclude? Is the Law identical with sin?" (7a). Since we believers are free from both the Law and sin, can we not consider both of them the same? Therefore, sin is the Law, and the Law is sin. "Certainly not!" Paul immediately responds. The Law defines sin: "Nevertheless, if it had not been for the Law, I should not have recognized sin or have known its meaning. [For instance] I would not have known about covetousness [would have had no consciousness of sin or sense of guilt] if the Law had not [repeatedly] said, You shall not covet and have an evil desire [for one thing and another]" (7b).

The Law says, "Thou shalt not covet" (*KJV*, Ex. 20.17a). Does knowing this Law stop us from coveting when we spot someone who has something we want? No! In fact, the Law magnifies our problem. "But sin, finding opportunity in the commandment [to express itself], got a hold on me *and* aroused *and* stimulated all kinds of forbidden desires (lust, covetousness). For without the Law, sin is dead . . . . But when the commandment came, sin lived again, and I died—was sentenced by the Law to death" (7.8-9).

What the Law does in the supreme courtroom of the universe is to provide mounds of evidence against us for our accuser. You and I may feel that we have been "pretty good" about keeping the Law, but that does not count in court. How we feel and perceive ourselves does not carry weight against the Law. If we have broken one small part of the Law, we may as well have broken all of it: "Cursed is the man who does not uphold the words of this law by carrying them out" (Deut. 27.26a). "And the very legal ordinance which was designed *and* intended to bring life, actually proved [to mean to me] death. For sin, seizing the opportunity *and* getting a hold on me [by taking its incentive] from the commandment, beguiled *and* entrapped *and* cheated me, and using it [as a weapon] killed me" (Rom. 7.10-11). The Law used the commandments to destroy me.

Remember: Mr. Law is holy. Do not try to pick him apart by looking for his faults. There are none. "The Law therefore is holy, and [each] commandment is holy and just and good. Did that which is good then prove fatal (bringing death) to me? Certainly not! It was sin, working death in me by using this good thing [as a weapon], in order that through the commandment sin might be shown up clearly to be sin . . ." (7.12-13). Sin and the weakness of the flesh are the culprits. Temptation knocks us down and the Law beats us up. The Law repeats, "You shall not covet. You shall not covet . . ." The next thing we know, we are begging for forgiveness for something for which the Law is now accusing us. The Law has no power to help us fulfill its requirements. When you are driving your car and you come to a stop sign, who must apply the brakes? The sign (Law) commands you to stop, but you must apply the power to stop.

The Bible is God's written plan of redemption; thus, it should never be used as a tool to beat someone over the head, not even oneself. The Law is useful to lead us to Christ. The Law follows behind us and nips us whenever we make one little misstep. If we run to Christ, we will be restored, not condemned. Remember, Mr. Law is alive and well; however, we are no longer obligated to Mr. Law—not even for negotiations. Praise the Lord!

How do we, then, differentiate between conviction and condemnation of sin? Spirit-inspired conviction leads to life, whereas Law-inspired condemnation leads to death. Conviction will bring attention to the areas of our lives where God wants to cut away the self and sin that would ruin us. Conviction, like surgery, hurts because our feelings are involved, but it leads to life and joy. Condemnation leads to depression and, finally, death.

THE LAW CANNOT JUSTIFY

The Law cannot justify us because it cannot deliver us from sin in our flesh. Saint Paul's confession confirms this vital truth, "For that which I do I allow not: for what I would, that do I not; but what I hate, that do I" (*KJV*, Rom. 7.15). The great missionary saint, Paul, is tempted to do what he despises and does not do what he desires. Why? "For I know that in me (that is, in my flesh,) dwelleth no good thing: for to will is present with me; but *how* to perform that which is good I find not. For the good that I would I do not: but the evil which I would not, that I do. Now if I do that I would not, it is no more I that do it, but sin that dwelleth in me" (*KJV*, 7.18-19). Paul has truly summed up the inner conflict of the man who is still on the road to the full revelation of Romans 7.1-6. The struggle is there. What is our natural response? We run to Mr. Law and plead, "Oh, Mr. Law, I am so sorry. Please, forgive me! I didn't mean to do it." Give it up. Mr. Law can't help us because our union with him is dissolved. Mr. Law is obligated to deal out judgment; Jesus Christ desires to minister grace. Let's embrace Jesus when we find ourselves tempted to sin. Like the little girl said, "When I get spanked by my mother, I hold tight to her waist and she can't get a good swing with her hand!"

Imagine a woman who was married to a man for fifteen years. This woman's husband daily isolated her, and abused her physically and emotionally. Then her dreadful husband died. She is suddenly free. Soon, she decides to marry another man who truly loves her. How long do you think she will retain the bad memories of her former spouse? Will all of the memory changes miraculously take place at the altar when she vows, "I do"? No! It will take some time to change her thinking. That is why Paul writes in chapter 12 of Romans that we must be transformed by the continual renewing of our minds.

The unhappy and pitiable person described in verses 15 through the end of chapter 7 is the person who still lives with flashbacks of the past marriage to Mr. Law. The conflict between the righteous actions you now desire and the questionable actions you are still tempted to do is the confusion caused by "yielding" to your flesh instead of embracing the freedom found in intimacy with Jesus. Condemnation comes to a heart still trying to please Mr. Law, not a heart full of faith in Jesus Christ. You were issued your death certificate at baptism. Move quickly away from your former miserable state of existence, "O wretched man that I am" (*KJV*, 24a), and go on to confess, "I thank God through Jesus Christ" (*KJV*, 25a).

Instead of trying to please the Law, obey the promptings of the Holy Spirit. Love Jesus Christ and live to please Him. He has already satisfied the demands of the Law (Matt. 5.17). The Law will always look for opportunities to inject condemnation, but Jesus is always looking for opportunities to inject grace. Our security is not in the Law. Our security is in the everlasting covenant commitment of His love relationship with us. May you live "happily ever after" in His grace! Amen.

**OUR SECURITY IS NOT IN THE LAW.
OUR SECURITY IS IN THE COVENANT COMMITMENT
OF HIS LOVE RELATIONSHIP WITH US.**

When Jesus cleans you up, He does it in a way that does not leave reminders to condemn us. Before I was married, I spent much time with printer's ink and auto grease. This made my nails black with motor oil and ink. My wife-to-be told me she did not want me to have dirty fingernails at our wedding. In order to solve my problem, I took a bottle of bleach and put each finger in it until the bleach ate out the dirt. My fingernails looked clean, but was my wife surprised, when she smelled bleach as I stood next to her at the altar. In Christ there is no permanent "smell" left when His blood cleanses you from all unrighteousness.

Chapter 21
LIFE IN UNION WITH THE HOLY SPIRIT

The end of Romans chapter 7 declares who will meet the challenge, which is similar to the endings of chapters 4, 5, 6, and 8. Each closing points to Jesus Christ our Lord. Romans chapter 4 verse 24 focuses on "Jesus our Lord" who was raised from the dead for the justification of all who believe. It is "Jesus Christ, the Messiah, the Anointed One, our Lord" (5.21) by Whom grace reigns through righteousness. "Jesus Christ our Lord" (6.23) provides eternal life as a free gift. Who will rescue you from your dying body? "Jesus Christ, the Anointed One, our Lord" (7.25) is the One to know. If anyone wants more good news, chapter 8 closes with the promise that "neither height nor depth, nor anything else in all creation, will be able to separate us from the love of God that is in Christ Jesus our Lord" (*NIV*, 8.39).

Thus far, only flawless Mr. Law has been introduced. However, Mr. Law has lots of relatives. The author of Romans introduces three more Laws in verse 23 of chapter 7: "But I discern in my bodily members . . . a different law (rule of action) at war against the law of my mind . . . making me a prisoner to the law of sin that dwells in my bodily organs . . . ." Good "Mr. Law" of God (22) is still alive and well and is now working with "a different law," the "law of my mind," and the "law of sin." Law always breeds more laws. In fact, the original commandments were only ten, but in order to make sure each detail of everyday life was covered, the Levitical laws were expanded to six hundred and thirteen.

In order to simplify matters, Jesus Christ introduces one simple law to supersede the old: "the law of the Spirit of life" (8.2).

Jesus' new Law of the Spirit frees those who believe from all of the old condemning laws like the "law of sin and death" spoken of in verse 2. Wait! In chapter 7 it was called "the law of sin;" now it is referred to as "the law of sin and death." Sin always leads to death!

The original story of when God gave the Ten Commandments to mankind is in Exodus 32. When Moses came down from the mountain with the Law in his hand, he saw the people dancing wildly, half-naked and out of control. In anger, Moses threw the tables of the Law down. As a result of the chaos, about 3,000 people died that awful day. To understand what the Law does, just look at its "birthday" present. The Law arrived and many died. The Law produced death starting from day one!

In the New Testament, the book of Acts records the history of how God poured out His Spirit in the upper room. On the day of Pentecost, a new "Spirit of life" descended upon the disciples. The recipients then stepped outside into the thronging multitudes. Peter began to preach in the power of this fresh spiritual anointing. God gave a new and different "birthday" present when about three thousand people were saved and made alive. The Spirit produces life! Which birthday gift do you prefer: the law—death, or the Spirit—life?

WHICH BIRTHDAY GIFT DO YOU PREFER: THE LAW—DEATH, OR THE SPIRIT—LIFE!

The Law produces death every time, because the Law is never satisfied. Conversely, the Spirit always produces life. The Spirit enables us to live a new lifestyle of joy, power, and victory. Hallelujah!

THE SPIRIT HAS SET US FREE FROM THE LAW

"Your Honor, Chapter 8 is the believer's spiritual 'bill of rights.'" He quotes, "For the law of the Spirit of life in Christ Jesus hath made me free from the law of sin and death" (*KJV*, Rom. 8.2). Jesus Christ has brought us personally out of the old life and into a brand-new lifestyle. Now, I think positively as I am being lifted and gifted by the Spirit of God.

God uses one law to trump another law. Just as the law of aerodynamics overcomes the law of gravity, so does the law of the Spirit of life overcome the law of sin and death. In the eighth chapter of Romans, the splendor of the contrast becomes most striking. Those who believe have emerged from the seventh chapter, with its accompanying failure and defeat, into the triumph of the Holy Spirit's victory through Jesus Christ.

"For God has done what the Law could not do, [its power] being weakened by the flesh . . . Sending His own Son in the guise of sinful flesh and as an offering for sin, [God] condemned sin in the flesh—subdued, overcame, deprived it of its power . . ." (8.3). Now, instead of us being condemned, sin has been condemned in us. God has made a failure-proof way for us to live life in a new way.

Chapter 8 is the cornerstone of true Christian liberty. It begins with the promise of "no condemnation . . . for those who are in Christ Jesus" and ends with another promise of no "separation . . . in Christ Jesus our Lord." In between there is no defeat! With promises like these, there is no room for depression. Think about it. We cannot lose with God. God does not condemn us, and we do not have to worry about a nasty divorce from Father God. Without the Spirit of life, it would be impossible for any person to be involved in ministry today. Therefore, let us allow Him to work—be flexible, be yielded—flow with His will.

FREE FROM CONDEMNATION

"Therefore, there is now no condemnation for those who are in Christ Jesus . . . For what the law was powerless to do in that it was weakened by the sinful nature, God did by sending his own Son in the likeness of sinful man to be a sin offering. And so he condemned sin in sinful man, in order that the righteous requirements of the law might be fully met in us" (*NIV*, 8.1 and 3-4a).

Since your Defense presented His case, the Judge now reads your new bill of rights. Agree out loud with what God decrees. That does not mean some apologies are not owed or restitution for wrongs is not appropriate, but really your debt is paid; you owe nothing, you are free. We make restitution out of love, not out of obligation to the Law. Now go on and live life by the Spirit of God. When you do, you will not find yourself living in the doldrums of Christian experience. We who believe are called to be eagles that move out in graceful, effortless flight. In fact, the winds of circumstances can lift eagles to higher heights when the eagles turn their wings to catch the warm wind currents.

CONDEMNATION AND JUDGMENT

What kinds of storms bring a believer down? One dark storm is a judgmental attitude. Circumstances swirl scarily around, and it is someone else's fault. If you and I have a judgmental attitude, we will live in condemnation because we not only misjudge others, but we also misjudge ourselves (Matt.7.1-5). You and I are really free from judgments in Christ Jesus. Whenever we find ourselves in the firestorm of judgment and condemnation, we must yield to the conviction of the Holy Spirit and soar above the conflict.

Paul records the believers' legal summation in Romans 8.1-3. He established in chapter 5 that as a believer, I am free from the wrath of God and delivered from the penalty of sin. When I am forgiven the devil has no legal right to demand payment for what I have done. My debt is paid in full. His conclusion repeats this most important fact with the written words: "THEREFORE [there is] now no condemnation—no adjudging guilty of wrong—for those who are in Christ Jesus . . ." He explains the reason in chapter 6 and again in verse 2 of chapter 8, "For the law of the Spirit of life [which is] in Christ Jesus . . . has freed me from the law of sin and of death." The believer's problem with sin is taken care of in Christ Jesus. The believer should have no struggle with the Law either: "For God has done what the Law could not do . . ." (8.3). The death of Jesus Christ has set us free from the wrath of God, sin, and the Law.

WALK AFTER THE SPIRIT

The theme of chapter 8 is "walk not after the flesh, but after the Spirit" (*KJV*, 1b and 4b). Why? "So that the righteous *and* just requirement of the Law might be fully met in us" (4a). The righteousness of the Law cannot be fulfilled in us when we try to produce it in our own flesh. It is fulfilled in us only as we yield to the Holy Spirit (Gal. 5.25b).

Does the following scenario remind you of yourself? The pressures of the world are on your life all the time. You stumble and fall out of step with the Spirit. The devil and sometimes well-meaning people accuse you saying, "You are a failure." You agree. The devil continues to throw judgments and accusations at you. After the resurrection of Jesus, the devil is known by the name "accuser of our brethren" (see Rev. 12.10). His full-time job is to bring charges against believers. Even when his accusing charges are true, they have no power over a believer's life. His purpose is to wear us down. He has NO power, unless we give it to him. As the earth has a gravitational pull downward, an object requires something greater to be interposed to defy that gravity. So also, the accuser tries to pull us downward, the greater law of grace defies that pull. As long as we continue to stand in the "batter's box" of salvation, we may continue swinging the bat as He teaches us to walk after the Spirit.

Trusting in Christ is like sitting in a large airplane. Some people are unsure of air safety and stir up enough courage to board a plane but never relax during flight. These passengers fear their full weight plus luggage will somehow cause the plane to crash.

The power of liftoff soon overcomes the passengers' fears and up into the sky they travel. The law of aerodynamics supersedes the law of gravity. Oftentimes the plane flies through rough weather. The lightening may flash and hailstones hit the fuselage. An inexperienced passenger may think, "It sure is dangerous in here. If only I could get out." Above the earth at about 37,000 feet in the midst of a storm is no place to bail out! This is the time to stay in your place, tighten your seatbelt, and trust in the pilot's ability. The pilot needs no help from you! He has seen worse storms than your present situation.

On the other hand, more experienced passengers know how to rest in the storm. Not only do these passengers snuggle into their seats, but they also ask for a pillow before falling asleep. Like babies in their mothers' arms, so are believers who have learned the secret of resting in Christ during the storms of life. They have put their full trust and confidence in God. The words of songwriter Frances Ridley Havergal's song "Like a River Glorious" ring true, "Those who trust Him wholly find Him wholly true." Trust breeds confidence and confidence produces rest.

TRUST BREEDS CONFIDENCE AND CONFIDENCE PRODUCES REST.

Now, no matter how much more evidence tries to be introduced into the eternal court, the supreme Judge has made up His mind about the verdict. Full justice has been provided through the One who stood with nail-scarred hands and said, "I paid it *all*."

PATTERNS OF BEHAVIOR

Although we are free in our new life in Christ Jesus, we may still have to break old, established ruts and patterns of behavior. "Therefore, brethren, we are debtors, not to the flesh, to live after the flesh. For if ye live after the flesh, ye shall die: but if ye through the Spirit do mortify the deeds of the body, ye shall live" (*KJV*, Rom. 8.12-13). To "mortify" is the process of putting to death.

There is a continual denying and putting to death the temptations of the flesh and the rules of the past.

Unlike the unique complete justification for which our Lord died to give us, this putting to death takes time. This putting off does not separate us from our union with our Lord's death; instead, it establishes and reaffirms our union with the Spirit of life as we continuously submit to the Spirit of life and turn from the sins of the flesh.

Our new life in Christ is often affected by our old behavior patterns. Whenever we are threatened, we tend to revert back into our old habit patterns. The new creature may step into an old creation rut. The new creation is not made to travel down old ruts. We are now children of God. The moment we misstep, our new nature cries out for the paths of righteousness. We need to develop new pathways in our spiritual walk. When old habits try to work on us, we have a new way of dealing with them—obey the Spirit's promptings.

In your new life, when something bad happens at a particular holiday, it may trigger your old ways of dealing with problems. Your old life beckons you! You feel "familiar" feelings. Now the Spirit in you renews your faith, and you yield to Christ rather than take a step backwards.

When someone becomes a new creature in Christ Jesus, does God destroy the barroom where he or she drank? Of course not. Old people, places, and times can remind us of the old life; they do not evaporate. The memories are still there, and they may trigger old dead feelings. The old life is past, but some of the old symbols may be still around. I am now born-again into the new life of Jesus Christ, a life lived not in my own feelings and strength, "but by the faith of the Son of God who loved me and gave Himself for me" (Gal. 2.20).

Since we have a whole new way of life in the Spirit, we must stay in fellowship with other members of the Body of Christ, in place of past sinful relationships. In the Spirit we freely accept and yield to the promptings of the Spirit of God, instead of the commandments of the Law: "Thou shall not . . . ," which arouse the forbidden in us. I have no power in myself; however, I am led and empowered by the Holy Spirit of God. To all who receive Him, He gives the power to become the children of God (Jn. 1.12).

RESPONDING TO THE SPIRIT'S LEADING

The power of a promise is in the Promise Giver, not the promise receiver. The best part is the power is in Jesus, the Promise Giver! When we have Him, we need not fear the commandments for He amazingly fulfills them through us for His glory.

THE BEST PART IS THE POWER IS IN JESUS, THE PROMISE GIVER!

Many Christians continue to live under the Law, and because it is never satisfied, they have no joy. If these same people were living by promptings of the Holy Spirit, He would lead them to choose what is right and avoid what is wrong, exchanging fear for joy. As we identify with His death and resurrection and accept our union with Him, He transfers His power to us. It may take time to operate in this new way because our minds must be renewed and new thought patterns established.

When Christ died for us, He paid the price in full. Subsequently, He returned to His Father in heaven, to make intercession and intervene for us (Heb. 7.25). The promptings of the Spirit are vital in our lives. When God's Spirit prompts your spirit to action, do it! You absolutely cannot walk in newness of life by yourself! It is His Spirit in you Who walks through you. The finished work of Jesus Christ on the Cross, and His present ministry at the right hand of the Father enables you to walk in newness of life. Deliverance from sin comes not by continually struggling to subdue the flesh, but by continually yielding to the Holy Spirit to renew and transform you.

Fear God more than sin. Pray daily for the Lord to lead and guide you. When He shows you something ugly from your old life unlike Himself, give it to Him. He can handle all our failures and weaknesses. Mr. Law is no longer in control of the new Person. We have married the One Who actually helps us in handling all of life's problems. He buried our old sins in the Father's sea of forgetfulness and put up a sign which reads "no fishing." When we understand who Jesus really is, we see that being joined to Him is totally different than being married to the old taskmaster Mr. Law. Jesus is gentle and long-suffering. The crown of Romans 8 is the One and only important Person—Jesus Christ our Lord.

When God's Spirit prompts your spirit to action, do it!

The words of the song "And Can It Be That I Should Gain," by Charles Wesley, shed redeeming light on the full salvation Christ purchased for us on Calvary.

Long my imprisoned spirit lay
Fast bound in sin and nature's night;
Thine eye diffused a quickening ray,
I woke, the dungeon flamed with light:
My chains fell off, my heart was free,
I rose, went forth, and followed Thee.

No condemnation now I dread,
Jesus, and all in Him, is mine;
Alive in Him, my living Head,
And clothed in righteousness divine,
Bold I approach the eternal throne,
And claim the crown, through Christ my own.

— *Charles Wesley*

Chapter 22

THE GODHEAD IN UNITY FOR OUR FREEDOM: NOT GUILTY! CASE CLOSED

True Christian freedom requires personal daily cooperation with all three Persons of the Godhead—the Father, the Son, and the Holy Spirit. The Godhead was functioning in unity in the first creation story; now Romans 8 shows all three clearly working together in the new creation of each saint. All three Persons are present in verses 3 and 4, "For what the law could not do, in that it was weak through the flesh, *God* sending his own *Son* in the likeness of sinful flesh, and for sin, condemned sin in the flesh: That the righteousness of the law might be fulfilled in us, who walk not after the flesh, but after the *Spirit*" (*KJV*). The Godhead is fully involved in the process of creating our new lives. God the Father, God the Son, and God the Holy Spirit have purchased our full redemption and freedom.

The three Persons of the Godhead are together again in verses 8 and 9, "So then they that are in the flesh cannot please *God* [the Father]. But ye are not in the flesh, but in the [Holy] Spirit, if so be that the [Holy] *Spirit* of God dwell in you. Now if any man have not the Spirit of [Jesus] *Christ*, he is none of his" (brackets added, *KJV*). The Godhead seals, confirms, undergirds, and strengthens our new-found freedom. With this truth in mind, we need not fear or falsely accuse any Person of the Godhead of condemning us. Satan and his followers deserve full credit for deceiving and accusing.

All three Persons appear together again in verse 11: "But if the [Holy] *Spirit* of him [the Father] that raised up *Jesus* [Christ] from the dead dwell in you, he [the Father] that raised up [Jesus] Christ from the dead shall also quicken your mortal bodies by his [Holy] *Spirit* that dwelleth in you" (brackets added, *KJV*).

Finally, if three times were not enough, then four times should be more than enough to reveal the oneness of the Trinity in chapter 8. Verses 16 and 17 state: "The [Holy] *Spirit* himself testifies with our spirit that we are *God's* [the Father's] children. Now if we are children, then we are heirs—heirs of God [the Father] and co-heirs with [Jesus] *Christ* . . ." (brackets added, *NIV*).

"Your Honor," we ask, "who can possibly be against us?"

Looking at the whole of chapter 8 of Paul's letter for the answer, we find the Godhead unanimously always for us. Our freedom is assured. "What then shall we say to [all] this?" (31a). Let us repeat what God has promised: "If God be for us, who [can be] against us?—Who can be our foe, if God is on our side?" (31b).

Meanwhile, here I stand in the divine courtroom overwhelmed by His tremendous forgiveness and redeeming evidence. The Judge has accepted the new evidence to cancel all my sins. A warm and gentle Spirit comes over me convicting me of just how exceedingly sinful my sin is (Rom. 7.13), and, at the same time, convincing me of the full revelation of the atonement made by Jesus Christ that took away my sin.

You might discouragingly argue, "God showed me something very bad in my life." Did He show you so you can be condemned by the devil's accusations? Or, did He show you in order for you to repent and give thanks for His great provision to forgive your sin? It is for the latter reason. Give thanks for the provision of the Cross! God was harder on His Son than He is on you because His Son took your sin and paid the full penalty on the Cross.

BODY, SOUL, AND SPIRIT

Created in the image of God, man was made body, soul, and spirit (three in one). After the fall of man recorded in Genesis, man's spirit died and was separated from God. Now there are two divisions of people in the world: saved people and unsaved people. The unsaved person's spirit is dead toward God because he or she is alienated by sin. This person has a living body and soul but is dead spiritually. You may see an unsaved person looking pretty "normal" using his or her body, mind, will, emotions, and ambitions. However, they lack a spiritual dimension towards God.

On the other hand, you may see a saved person looking pretty "normal," too. This person uses his or her body, mind, will, emotions, and ambitions, but for very different purposes than the unsaved person. The saved, born-again person's spirit is made alive by the Holy Spirit Who lives within, for ". . . if any one does not possess the (Holy) Spirit of Christ, he is none of His—he does not belong to Christ [is not truly a child of God]" (8.9b). The saved person has the divine ability to live victoriously in this present world because the dynamite Spirit of God has made His home in this person. The Holy Spirit breathes life and purpose into this person's mind, will, emotions, ambitions, and body to create a holy life purpose and destiny.

FIVE SENSES CONTACT THE WORLD

There are some people who live only for their bodily appetites like food, sex, pleasure, drugs, and the like. Whatever affects their physical bodies is the most important part of their lives. In fact, their minds function to serve their bodily cravings that connect them to the world through their five senses. People who are led by five natural senses respond to the outside world first because it has direct contact to their bodies. Instead of being Spirit-led from the inside out, these persons are led from the outside in. Their world-infected bodies try to feed their unfulfilled souls. This kind of backward-functioning person seeks chemicals administered through the body first to maintain a meager existence.

VICTORY THROUGH THE POWER OF THE SPIRIT

Yielding to the power of the Spirit is the only way to victory in Jesus Christ. Remember the great conflict Paul described in chapter 7 of Romans? You and I try to do the right thing, but we fail. What a strain this conflict puts in our lives. We find ourselves buried in verses like "O unhappy *and* pitiable *and* wretched man that I am!" (Rom.7.24a).

Since chapter 7 describes the conflict, chapter 8 records the victory. Verses 1 through 11 reveal the power of the Holy Spirit Who is on our side. Verses 12 through 17 assert our sonship. The Holy Spirit witnesses to us that we are indeed children of God Who already won the war. We inherit His victory through relationship with Him. Verses 18 through 30 assure us that even suffering does not affect our victorious position because the Spirit holds us firm. If you are sick or suffering, do not think that God is punishing you. God loves you even when you pass through His discipline (Heb.12.5-7). In fact, the Father's discipline in your life is evidence that you are his son or daughter. He is doing in your life more than what your circumstances indicate.

Romans 8.28 is a spiritual blanket that covers all things: ". . . all things work together *and* are [fitting into a plan] for good to those who love God and are called according to [His] design *and* purpose." When I was a child, my mother made a chocolate cake from scratch. When she wasn't looking I ate a piece of her Baker's bitter chocolate and immediately spit it out. I had assumed that the final product, a sweet chocolate cake, contained only sweet ingredients. I was wrong. Similarly, the sweet result God has in mind for our lives includes some bitter ingredients. In the end these bittersweet experiences work together for our good, making us more into the image of His dear Son.

Finally, verses 31 through 39 record His written guarantee of victory by the Spirit.

THE SPIRIT-LED LIFE

Romans chapter 8 focuses on the Spirit-led person. The focus shifts from *I* in chapter 7 to *spirit* in chapter 8. In the Amplified Bible, the word *I* appears thirty-four times in chapter 7 and the word *spirit* appears twenty-nine times in chapter 8. The death of I is recorded at the end of chapter 7: "O unhappy *and* pitiable *and* wretched man that I am! Who will release *and* deliver me from [the shackles of] this body of death? O thank God!—He will!" (24-25a). The life of the Spirit comes with the guarantee described at the end of chapter 8: ". . . neither death, nor life, nor angels, nor principalities, nor things impending *and* threatening, nor things to come, nor powers, Nor height, nor depth, nor anything else in all creation will be able to separate us from the love of God which is in Christ Jesus our Lord" (38b-39).

A mature Spirit-led person is one who has submitted mind, spirit, and body to the control of the Holy Spirit. He or she lives in contact with the world through the five natural senses, but the Holy Spirit living within filters out any wrong body-led or soul-led stimuli that contradict His Will.

For instance, when King David wrote, "Bless the Lord, O my soul: and all that is within me, *bless* his holy name" (*KJV*, Ps. 103.1), his soul was receiving its directive from the Holy Spirit—from the inside out. Likewise, when we receive our directives from the Spirit, He enables us to "bless the Lord" in every circumstance. Our living becomes an act of worship as our spirit yields to the Holy Spirit and we begin to worship. Our bodies may follow with clapping, dancing or uplifted hands, etc. Our bodies respond to the impulses that come by the Spirit. Our old natures took orders from our souls and bodies. God wants to turn us inside out so our control center is His Spirit, which makes us alive body, soul, and spirit.

GOD WANTS TO TURN US INSIDE OUT SO OUR CONTROL CENTER IS HIS SPIRIT, WHICH MAKES US ALIVE BODY, SOUL, AND SPIRIT.

What does a Spirit-led life look like? The Spirit beautifies and strengthens our emotions. He relaxes our bodies and makes our spirits alive. We are whole people only as we yield to His Spirit. Do not allow your body or soul to direct your life by yielding to its cravings and desires. Invite the Spirit to lead and keep connected to the whole Body of Christ.

Acts 2.4 records the Holy Spirit's arrival upon the united believers. Their bodies were affected when they "... began to speak in other (different, foreign) languages, as the Spirit kept giving them clear *and* loud expression ...." The day of Pentecost affected them—body, soul and spirit!

You or I do not naturally have the power to live a victorious Christian life. When we allow the supernatural power of the Holy Spirit to control us, He will accomplish God's purpose in us beyond human possibilities. If we walk by the Spirit, we will not fulfill the lusts of the flesh (Gal. 5.16). The plain truth is that those who "live in accordance with the Spirit have their minds set on what the Spirit desires" (*NIV*, Rom. 8.5b).

How do we practically live daily in accordance with the Spirit? Die to sinful, fleshly impulses. You and I are not obligated to obey our sinful natures (8.12). We have the power to separate ourselves from sin. Each day, as temptation to do wrong comes to your mind, submit your spirit to the Father and relax in His strong grip. He will not hurt you. He will protect and empower you.

Only in Christ can we resist the devil and the flesh. The devil will not give up accusing us in God's courtroom every time we mess up; however, in Christ we are able to humbly repent of our failure because we know Jesus has set us legally free from punishment (see 1 John 1.7 and 9).

Does being led by the Spirit mean we will never sin? Of course not! We will fail and sin. Being led by the Spirit means "If we [freely] admit that we have sinned *and* confess our sins, He is faithful and just . . . and will forgive our sins (dismiss our lawlessness) and continuously cleanse us from all unrighteousness—everything not in conformity to His will in purpose, thought and action" (1 Jn. 1.9). Furthermore, "if any one should sin, we have an Advocate (One Who will intercede for us) with the Father; [it is] Jesus Christ [the all] righteous—upright, just, Who conforms to the Father's will in every purpose, thought and action" (1 Jn. 2.1b). The Father has made full provision for us, even regarding our failures. Our victory is not based on our acceptance of feelings; it is based on the Father's perfectly executed plan of salvation in Christ Jesus.

THE TRINITY IS FOR US

"What shall we say to all these things?" (*NKJV*, Rom. 8.31). The whole Trinity—Father, Son, and Holy Spirit—is for us. That is why Paul writes through the inspiration of the Holy Spirit, "If God be for us, who [can be] against us?—Who can be our foe, if God is on our side?" (Rom. 8.31b).

Is it possible that one of the three Persons of the Trinity might turn against us? What an absurd thought in light of the fact we were bought not with silver or gold but "[you were purchased with] the precious blood of Christ" (1 Pet. 1.19a). "He who did not withhold *or* spare [even] His own Son but gave Him up for us all" (8.32a). God is for us one hundred percent at all times in order to "freely *and* graciously give us all [other] things" (8.32b). His love for us will never change. Not only has He forgiven us but He continues to give us everything His own Son died to purchase for us—EVERYTHING. Cross God's name off your list of possible accusers.

Paul records the Judge's question, "Who *is* he that condemneth?" (*KJV*, 8.34a).

Is he Jesus Christ? No! Jesus cannot possibly be the one who condemns us and "Who died, or rather Who was raised from the dead, Who is at the right hand of God actually pleading as He intercedes for us" (8.34b). Therefore, it is impossible for Jesus Christ to be the one who accuses, condemns, depresses, and blackmails you and me. In fact, He is doing just the opposite—He, at this very moment, is making intercession as our lawyer before the Father on our behalf.

"Who is he that condemneth?" (*KJV*, 8.34a). Is he the Holy Spirit? The apostle Paul established in verses 26 and 27 that the Holy Spirit ". . . comes to our aid *and* bears us up in our weakness . . . because the Spirit intercedes *and* pleads [before God] in behalf of the saints according to *and* in harmony with God's will." It is a contradiction to intercede and plead for people while, at the same time, condemning them. Confess out loud what God the Father, Jesus Christ, and the Holy Spirit have done and are presently doing on your behalf.

God is for me. He loves me. He has my back. He goes before me. He will never accuse me. I am His in three ways: I have been born into His family (Jn. 3.3), I have been adopted into His family (Eph. 1.5), and I am His bride (Rev. 19.7 and 9).

At the end of chapter 8 of the *King James Version* of the Bible, there is a list of seventeen common ills and obstacles that plague mankind—miseries like tribulation, persecution, famine, sword, and death. The believer cannot use any one of these obstacles as an excuse, nor fear any of these ills because nothing "else in all creation, will be able to separate us from the love of God that is in Christ Jesus our Lord" (8.39). Do not allow circumstances to divorce you from the Father's love. We are free to live in God's love every day despite our failures or successes.

The Supreme Judge has heard all the evidence and arguments. Our Defense Lawyer now asks, **"Your Honor,** what is your final verdict?" The Judge, having given His opinion, now asks the defendants to stand. The gavel falls. The Judge declares to all present, ***"Not guilty!"*** and His words reverberate throughout eternity. The courtroom breaks forth in resounding praise. All sinners who accept the sacrifice of their Advocate, the One with nail-scarred hands are not guilty and nothing will separate them from God's love, which is in Christ Jesus. And we cannot be tried again for the same crime. Case closed! All praise be to our Defense Attorney, our Lord and Savior, forever and ever! Amen.

WE ARE FREE BY HIS DIVINE DECREE!

Part V

THE SOVEREIGNTY OF GOD

Chapter 23
GOD'S CHOSEN PEOPLE

The sovereignty of God to the Jews is the theme of Romans chapters 9 through 11. The apostle Paul begins with the following heart-felt confession: "I am speaking the truth in Christ. I am not lying; my conscience [enlightened and prompted] by the Holy Spirit, bearing witness with me That I have bitter grief and incessant anguish in my heart. For I could wish that I myself were accursed *and* cut off *and* banished from Christ, for the sake of my brethren . . ." (Rom. 9.1-3).

The ache in Paul's heart was for the promises of God to Abraham to be shared by all of Israel. However, God's promises are only given to those who believe. For example, Christ is not slow in fulfilling His promises because He desires all people to "turn to repentance" (2 Pet. 3.9). Will all people, however, turn to repentance? No. The belief that all people will ultimately be saved is the erroneous belief of universalism. Although God desires all to be saved, only a remnant of people will believe and turn toward God in repentance. Likewise, His eternal promises made to a specific nation may not necessarily be received by the entire nation.

HEIRS OF FAITH

To properly understand God's promises to Israel, one needs to begin with Abraham. From Adam to Abraham there is no mention of a "special" people. There were only individuals whom God laid His hand upon. Finally, in Abraham, God found a unique individual who would live by faith and obedience, even to the offering of his promised son Isaac. Because of his faith, God promised

specifically identifies the Seed with the proper name "Christ, the Messiah." True Israel is the Seed of Abraham by faith in Jesus Christ. Any person in Christ becomes a part of true Israel by complete faith in the Seed. The Seed is also referred to prophetically in Gen. 3.15 where a Savior is promised to come.

There is some teaching of a national conversion in which all of Israel will be saved based upon Romans 11.26a. This teaching advocates that as the nation of Israel goes, so goes the timing of God's countdown of the last days. The Word of God, however, clearly emphasizes there is a real difference between natural Jews and "true" Jews. The distinction is not based on one's natural heritage, but rather on one's spiritual heritage through faith in Jesus Christ. Natural Jewish people belong to true Israel only when their obedience comes through their faith in the One sacrifice. God will have millions of people from all races and tribes who make up the "called out" ones—His redeemed people, His Church, and His bride (see Rev. 5.9).

In the Old Testament, the grace of God was demonstrated toward Gentiles, too. These Gentiles by obedience of faith were a part of "true" Israel, even though they were not naturally born Jews. For example, the harlot Rahab was saved by her faith. Ruth, a Moabitess, was taken also from the Gentiles and listed in the genealogy of the people of faith, and was one of the great-grandmothers of Jesus (see Matt. 1.5). Jesus Christ's death, burial, and resurrection changed EVERYTHING. There is an endless, consistent line of people from all nations and tribes who have received God's mercy and grace through faith in the Jewish Messiah—Jesus.

Paul quotes Isaiah as another source to build his case for a remnant. In Romans 9.27 through 29 he supports his thesis with borrowings from this trustworthy Old Testament Jewish prophet: ". . . Though the number of the sons of Israel be as the sand of the sea, only a remnant—a small part of them—will be saved [from perdition, condemnation, judgment] . . . If the Lord of hosts had not left us a seed . . . we (Israel) would have fared like Sodom and have been made like Gomorrah." The original promise given to

Abraham compared his seed to the number of stars in the sky (spiritual seed) and sand of the seashore (natural seed); however, as Isaiah points out, only a remnant (small number) of Abraham's natural seed will believe in the true Seed. This is important because it indicates Abraham will have an earthy (natural) seed and a heavenly (spiritual) seed. The Jews, the natural seed, will yet inherit the natural promises of the land. The spiritual promises are given to the true Israel through faith in Jesus the Messiah.

The Cross of Jesus Christ is the pivotal point that joins Jews and Gentiles into "members together of one body" (Eph. 3.6). As a result of the Cross, Gentile and Jewish believers who accept Jesus Christ the Messiah's sacrifice for their sins are all a part of true Israel.

In God's sight, the important separation is not along country lines or natural heritage. He draws a clear line between people who believe in Him and people who do not believe Him. It is a matter of believing His character as being trustworthy. God remembers His promises to the Jewish people, and He will not go back on His promises. His promise of a land is yet to take place in its entire glorious fulfillment (see Gal. 3.28 and Col. 3.11).

ONLY ONE WAY TO SALVATION

It is true that natural-born Jews do have certain privileges over Gentiles, according to Scripture. Paul names one advantage back in verse 2 of chapter 3: ". . . they have been entrusted with the very words of God" (*NIV*). More advantages are listed in chapter 9 verses 4 and 5: ". . . to them belong God's adoption [as a nation] and the glorious (Shekinah) Presence. With them were the special covenants made, to them was the Law given. To them [the temple] worship was revealed and [God's own] promises announced. To them belong the patriarchs, and as far as His natural descent was concerned from them is the Christ, Who is exalted *and* supreme over all, God, blessed forever! Amen—so let it be." However, the fact that people are given privileges, does not guarantee those privileges will be appropriated. Take, for example, Esau, who sold his privileged birthright for a dish of stew. What good did the firstborn birthright do for him? There are a myriad of others who could be named such as Cain, Korah, Saul, Jezebel, and even Judas Iscariot, who was privileged to be one of the original twelve disciples of Jesus. The greater the privileges bestowed, the greater the responsibility and judgment attached.

How, then, should true Israelites respond to natural Israel? We should identify with Paul who wrote, "BRETHREN, [with all] my heart's desire *and* goodwill for (Israel) I long and pray to God that they may be saved" (Rom. 10.1). We must pray because God wants to reveal His love to natural Jews and wants them to accept Christ the Messiah. God desires all men everywhere should be saved!

THE GREATER THE PRIVILEGES BESTOWED, THE GREATER THE RESPONSIBILITY AND JUDGMENT ATTACHED.

God honors faith in Him. All Jews and Gentiles who accept the Cross of Christ and continue to put their full trust in Jesus are included in God's family. "The Scripture says, No man who believes in Him—who adheres to, relies on and trusts in Him—will [ever] be put to shame or be disappointed. [No one,] for there is no distinction between Jew and Greek. The same Lord is Lord over all [of us] and He generously bestows His riches upon all who call upon Him [in faith]. For every one who calls upon the name of the Lord will be saved" (Rom. 10.11-13). According to Scripture there is in Christ no distinction between Jew and Gentile because Jesus broke down the middle wall of partition and made us all one (see Eph. 2.13-16).

After establishing the good news of unity between believing Jews and believing Gentiles, the author of Romans now poses a series of logical questions. How can people call for help to someone they do not know? How are nations going to hear about and believe in Jesus if no one tells them? How is anyone going to tell them unless they are sent? The answer to these questions is the reason for The Great Commission. The heathen will not benefit from the good news unless Christians reach and preach. "Missionaries" cannot preach unless they are sent. Paul concludes this point with a beautiful quotation from Isaiah once again: "How beautiful are the feet of those who bring glad tidings!—How welcome is the coming of those who preach the good news of His good things! (Isa. 52.7 and Rom. 10.15).

SALVATION IS ALWAYS PERSONAL.

Chapter 10 explains the basic plan of salvation that no one will be saved unless he or she calls upon the name of the Lord. This fact must be clearly established in order to withstand flawed teachings that may indicate there is another way for some to be saved. Only Christ's body in the world, His living organism made of those who have called on the name of the Lord, are saved.

GOD IS KEEPING A REMNANT

God brings judgment on persons and nations, but salvation is personal for "whosoever wills." Salvation is always personal. Paul quotes Elijah in Romans 11.3: "Lord, they have killed Your prophets, they have demolished Your altars, and I alone am left, and they seek my life." What does God confidently reply? "I have kept for Myself seven thousand men who have not bowed the knee to Baal!" (4b). Even though it looked to Elijah that he was the only one left, God saw the bigger picture which included thousands whom Elijah could not see.

Just as a remnant was preserved in Elijah's day, Paul writes, "So too at the present time there is a remnant (a small believing minority), selected (chosen) by grace . . ." (11.5).

In these last days, revivals worldwide are on the increase. The "privileged" natural Jews will witness what others are inheriting, violates His eternal principles. He alone is God, and He alone rules His creation. At the end of chapter 11, the apostle reminds his readers of the awesome sovereignty of God:

> "Oh, the depths of the riches of the wisdom and knowledge of God! How unsearchable His judgments, and His paths beyond tracing out! Who has known the mind of the Lord? Or who has been His counselor? Who has ever given to God, that God should repay him? For from Him and through Him and to Him are all things. To Him be glory forever! Amen." (*NIV*, Romans 11.33-36)

How supreme is God! He is the same yesterday today and forever. "To God Our Savior who alone is wise, be glory and majesty, dominion and power, both now and forever amen" (*NKJV*, Jude 25).

Chapter 24
CHRISTIAN CONSECRATION

Having been declared not guilty by the Supreme Judge in chapter 8 of Romans, the believing defendants step out of the courtroom free to live in this world. Now they must be shown how to live this free new life! *As each one yields to the Spirit, a strong godly foundation develops that makes for righteous character.* Our strong beliefs and character grow in the soil of everyday consecration and produce the godly fruit of righteousness. In chapter 12 of Romans, the apostle Paul turns the reader's attention to this new way of living. He begins with the principle of consecration in verses 1 and 2. He continues in verses 3 through 21 by describing what this consecration looks like in everyday life. He describes a life marked by humility and service (3-8), love toward other believers (9-13), and love toward all mankind, including persecutors (14-21).

The book of Romans may be sub-divided into three major sections. Each section is marked off by the word "therefore," which is used to make the reader stop and ponder what the word is "there for" in light of the prior teaching. Paul marks off the first major section in chapter 5, verse 1, when he writes, "THEREFORE, since we are justified—acquitted, declared righteous, and given a right standing with God—let us [grasp the fact that we] have [the peace of reconciliation] to hold and to enjoy, peace with God . . ." The first "therefore" marks off our *justification*, which brings peace and access to God.

"THEREFORE [there is] now no condemnation—no adjudging guilty of wrong—for those who are in Christ Jesus" (8.1a). The second "therefore" results in *sanctification*. What Christ has done, as described by Paul in chapters 6 and 7, purifies us from a guilty conscience and frees us from the Law. Condemnation by the Law has no place in our lives.

Finally, chapter 12, verse 1, marks the third major "THERE-FORE" section used to stop the reader for contemplation: "I appeal to you therefore, brethren, *and* beg of you in view of [all] the mercies of God, to make a decisive dedication of your bodies—presenting all your members and faculties—as a living sacrifice, holy (devoted, consecrated) and well pleasing to God, which is your reasonable (rational, intelligent) service *and* spiritual worship." This "therefore" requires *consecration* as our response to the rich mercies of God revealed in chapters 4 through 8.

RESPONSE OF CONSECRATION

In gratitude we offer ourselves to the Lord: "With eyes wide open to the mercies of God, I beg you, my brothers, as an act of intelligent worship, to give him your bodies, as a living sacrifice . . ." (*J.B. Phillips,* Rom.12.1). Focusing our eyes completely on His mercy evokes a love response. This supernatural love response is the presentation of our bodies as living sacrifices. This response is not possible when we focus on how much we are giving up or when we compare ourselves with friends, family, and other church members. We must concentrate fully on the mercies of God.

According to 1 Corinthians chapter 6 our bodies are the temples of the living God. The living Holy Spirit within enables us to present our natural bodies to God. This word *present* is a temple term meaning "to dedicate." In Romans 6.13 this same Greek word is rendered as *yield*. In response to Christ's great salvation, we are to present or yield our bodies to God. There may be a struggle between the Spirit within and the flesh without to present our bodies. Paul says, ". . . we have this treasure in earthen vessels, that the excellency of the power may be of God, and not of us" (*KJV*, 2

Cor. 4.7). We need to be reminded again, "THEREFORE [there is] now no condemnation . . ." (Rom. 8.1). Whenever the enemy of your soul tries to force you to go a crooked way, the Holy Spirit will remind you, "Just yield yourself to Me. Yield. That is all. Do not yield to the ways of the enemy, because I have freed you and given you the power and desire to choose my way."

Before we were saved, we had no choice in the matter. If the devil demanded, "Do this!" we found it impossible to resist because we were under his dominion. Now we have a choice. We will either offer our bodies to the devil by default or to God by choice. When we yield to God, we yield ourselves to the One with resurrection power. It is much more a "reasonable service" to offer one's body to God Who can raise the dead, than to the thief who comes "to steal and to kill and to destroy" (see Jn. 10.10).

Yielding our bodies to God is not only "an act of intelligent worship," but it is also "spiritual worship" (Rom. 12.1b). The offering of one's body to God is the highest form of worship because it is giving Him your whole three-part being to Him.

YOU ARE IN CHRIST

"Don't let the world around you squeeze you into its own mould" (*J.B. Phillips,* Rom.12.2a). We are being squeezed by the world into its mold, and for the most part we are not even aware of it. When I was a child, we mixed plaster and put it in a mold. After letting it dry, we took it out to see it had hardened to the shape of the mold. Likewise, the world wants to dictate your lifestyle. With the world's pressure on us, it is imperative we recognize our need to yield to His embrace instead of the world's influence. In John 17.15 Jesus said, "I pray not that thou shouldest take them out of the world, but that thou shouldest keep them from the evil." His purpose is insulation not isolation! The problem is that in our insecurity we try to fit into the world scene. We are aroused by the world's stimuli in our flesh, and we respond to it. The world jump on the plank to see if it would break. Sometimes a board would creak and crack. Only the plank that did not break was hoisted up on the roof to be trusted not to break when walked on. So it is with us. God tests us near the ground with small responsibilities to see whether or not we will stand the tests. If we do, He will give us greater responsibilities. His love keeps Him from placing us in a high position when He knows we would break and destroy the lives of those that look to us for leadership. Be faithful in the small details and God will give you greater responsibilities and influence.

Chapter 25
GIFTS OF THE SPIRIT

Stepping out of the courtroom into the sunlight of life presents a serious challenge to the new believer who has spent years in sin's grip. In order to adjust to this new freedom, we must present our bodies as living sacrifices. The Spirit will make His spiritual gifts available to us in order that we may live effectively for Christ every day. The seven God-given motivational gifts listed in Romans chapter 12 are compromised unless we first present our bodies as living sacrifices.

Another set of gifts is enumerated in 1 Corinthians 12. There, nine manifestation gifts are listed that operate in the Holy Spirit by love. The Corinthian list may be divided up into "vocal" gifts—tongues, interpretation, and prophecy; "power" gifts—miracles, faith, and healing; and "knowing" gifts—discerning of spirits, words of wisdom, and the word of knowledge. Pentecostals and Charismatics have traditionally focused on the Corinthian nine. These nine gifts are, however, built upon the Romans seven.

Eight additional gifts of ministry are listed in 1 Corinthians chapter 12. (See chart on facing page.) These three sets of gifts should be viewed as interactive and effective under the Lordship of Christ by the Holy Spirit.

FUNCTIONING WITHIN OUR GIFTS

Romans 12.4-6 uses the human body as an example for understanding the function of the gifts of the Spirit: "For as in one physical body we have many parts (organs, members) and all of these

GIFTS OF THE SPIRIT

Romans 12.3-8 MOTIVATIONAL GIFTS	**I Corinthians 12.27-31** MINISTRY GIFTS	**I Corinthians 12.7-11** MANIFESTATION GIFTS
PROPHECY (I COR. 14.1)	APOSTLES	**VOCAL:** TONGUES INTERPRETATIONS PROPHECY
SERVING (GAL. 5.13)	PROPHETS	**KNOWING:** KNOWLEDGE WISDOM DISCERNMENT
TEACHING (MATT. 28.20)	TEACHERS	**POWER:** HEALING MIRACLES FAITH
EXHORTING (HEB. 3.13)	MIRACLES	
GIVING (MATT. 10.8)	HEALINGS	
RULING (I TIM. 3.4)	HELPS	
MERCY (LK. 10.37)	GOVERNMENT	
	TONGUES	

parts do not have the same function *or* use, So we . . . are one body in Christ, the Messiah, and individually we are parts one of another . . . Having gifts (faculties, talents, qualities) that differ according to the grace given us, let us use them . . ." The gifts operate in much the same way as the human body functions. Each gift to the body has a specific purpose and function and is given to beautifully benefit the whole. They are not to impress through empty individualistic performance, which can lead to an exaggerated opinion of one's self. Gifts are for function more than beauty.

Some believers have the gift of prophecy: "[He whose gift is] prophecy, [let him prophesy] according to the proportion of his faith" (12.6b). Prophecy, speaking God's Word, functions properly only within the measure of the faith the person speaking has received. Faith and prophecy go hand-in-hand. Substance and evidence confirm prophecy. As we will learn later in this chapter, the purpose is the edification, exhortation, and comfort of the Church.

Other believers may have the gift of practical service: "[He whose gift is] practical service, let him give himself to serving" and still others are gifted teachers: "he who teaches, to his teaching" (12.7). Exhortation, giving, ruling, and mercy are the remaining essential motivational gifts. Sometimes I wonder why so many people seem to have the gift of "ruling" and so few the gift of "giving!"

EACH TO OPERATE IN ALL THE GIFTS

The seven gifts listed in Romans 12 are often referred to as "motivational" gifts. Because they are basic to defining each person, it is advantageous to be keenly aware of our gifts. Some who have the gift of serving are pastors. They pastor the church as a shepherd, leading the people by service. There are other believers who are motivated by the gift of ruling or administration. They lead the church through leadership and organization. All the gifts are needed for the Body of Christ to accomplish God's purposes.

Another exciting part of God's gifts is that the same person can sometimes function in different gifts. Although a gift may be given specifically to each person, God commands all of us to exercise our faith by operating to some degree in all of the motivational gifts as the need arises. For example, there are those in the Body of Christ who have the gift of giving. This does not mean that a person with the gift of prophecy is exempt from giving. Giving may not be the primary gift that comes to mind of a person with the gift of prophecy, but he or she is still expected to be a giver (Matt. 10.8). There is a great sovereign balance in the Body of Christ. When each of us is doing what God has called us to do, there will never be too many or too few functioning in one place and at one time. Do not be afraid to reach out and bless others. Get out of the box. God has specifically gifted individuals, but He also expects these gifts to be multiplied, renewed, and developed by use.

Let us take a closer look at the *gift of prophecy:* "Pursue love, yet desire earnestly spiritual gifts, but especially that you may prophesy" (*NASB*, 1 Cor. 14.1). Although prophecy is a gift given to certain persons in the Body of Christ, we are here all exhorted to desire to prophesy—speaking forth the Word of God. There are three levels to prophecy. First is the "Spirit of prophecy" that comes upon a corporate gathering of believers. Anyone in the meeting may speak because the Spirit is encouraging believers to exercise the prophetic gift. When the Spirit of prophecy is present in a service, even one who has not prophesied before is able to speak forth the word of the Lord in an orderly manner (see 1 Sam. 10.10-11). They may pray aloud or read a quickened scripture. The body is designed and "knit together by what every joint supplies . . ." (*NKJV*, Eph. 4.16).

A second function of the "gift of prophecy" occurs when the atmosphere or presence may not be conducive to the prophetic. In a corporate gathering, or in other situations, it may be that everybody has come together discouraged and hurting. A person present with the gift of prophecy when quickened by the Holy Spirit is able by faith to speak forth a powerful word of encouragement. The word may be as simple as reminding the believers to lift up their heads for the King of Glory will come in (Ps. 24.7, 9). The word encourages the listeners and builds their faith.

The third function of prophecy is the office of the prophet. This is one whose whole ministry and lifestyle makes a prophetic statement. Two clear examples of this office of prophet are the Old Testament's Jeremiah and the New Testament's John the Baptist. Their lifestyles were prophetic statements, declaring the message of the Lord by word and example.

God wants us all to be prophetic, that is, to speak forth the Word of God! First Corinthians 14.3 provides a tri-fold safety zone for prophecy practice. This "prophetic triangle" has three boundaries: edification, exhortation, and comfort. Spirit-filled believers who desire to exercise the gift of prophecy must observe these three clear boundaries. As the word stays within its God-given limitations/boundaries the hearers are safe. Believers must learn to discern a genuine prophetic message within the boundaries, as opposed to a word given from a carnal mind. The church leadership and elders are there to "judge all prophesies."

Words have the power of life and death (Prov. 18.21). Thus, the "vocal gifts" of prophecy, tongues, and interpretation have the strongest guidelines in order to prevent misuse. The apostle Paul spends three whole chapters in 1 Corinthians—12, 13, and 14—detailing the use and motive of these vocal gifts. These gifts are available for every believer, but they come with detailed safety instructions in the Owner's manual—the Bible. If violated, what was meant to be a blessing could become the source of confusion, conflict, and division.

God has made these gifts readily available because they are desperately needed. The body has a daily need for edification, for exhortation, and for comfort. Start practicing. Stay in the safety zone. Trust your church elders and leaders to help you learn to discern the certain from the uncertain and the true from the false.

Whenever you and I step out by faith into new territory, there is warfare. If you believe you have a prophetic word but feel doubtful, check with the church's leadership over you. Find out how your local church leadership wants you to safely exercise the gifts in your church or fellowship. We will learn through our mistakes and successes.

SERVING "AS UNTO THE LORD" ACCRUES DIVINE REWARDS . . .

Practical service is the next motivational gift listed (Rom. 12.7a). Some people readily confess, "I am a server," while others flout, "I'm glad I'm not a server." Everyone is called to serve according to Galatians 5.13, "For you, brethren, were [indeed] called to freedom . . . but through love you should serve one another." Furthermore, Colossians 3.23-24 (*KJV*) exhorts, "Whatsoever ye do, do it heartily, as to the Lord . . . for ye serve the Lord Christ." Whenever we serve in His name, we are truly serving Jesus Christ our Lord. Some have the motivational gift to serve, but everyone has opportunity for service. Always be ready to serve with the attitude of a good servant. Serving "as unto the Lord" accrues divine rewards "he who is greatest among you, shall be your servant" (*NKJV*, Matt. 23.11).

The *gift of teaching* is another motivational gift. However, if teaching is not your motivational gift, it does not mean God will never ask you to teach. If you are a parent or leader of children or adults, you will teach in word and example. Why not practice becoming an excellent teacher? Colossians 3.16 encourages all of us to help one another along on the right road with our psalms, hymns, and spiritual songs. Furthermore, Jesus Christ commissions all of us to teach ". . . everything that I have commanded you . . ." (Matt. 28.20). That large an order will take the whole body of Christ's participation full time.

Some believers are given to encouraging others: "(He who exhorts, encourages), to his *exhortation* . . ." (Rom. 12.8). Although some of us may not have the gift to encourage, we have a great responsibility to exhort our fellow believers. Hebrews exhorts all of us to encourage: "warn (admonish, urge and encourage) one another every day" (3.13a) and to urge: "admonishing—warning, urging, and encouraging—one another, and all the more faithfully as you see the day approaching" (10.25b). As our vertical relationship with God grows, so will our horizontal relationships with people. One fruit of growth is that of mutual exhortation. In order to motivate believers to greater things in God, a strong exhorting gift must be evident in the church encouraging everyone to excellence.

Sandwiched between encouragement and leadership is the blessed *gift of giving* (Rom. 12.13). No one is exempt from this gift. Giving is commanded over and over in the Bible. For instance, Jesus commands his disciples, "Freely (without pay) you have received; freely (without charge) give" (Matt. 10.8b) and "Give, and [gifts] will be given you, good measure, pressed down, shaken together and running over" (Lk. 6.38a). If we truly are a part of Christ's body, we should not say, "I don't have the gift of giving. Let those who have the gift give." He has joined all of His gifts together and no person has the right to pick and choose to suit themselves. If you think you have nothing to give, ask God who gives liberally. Giving may be a gift of the Spirit to some, but it must be an active, compassionate lifestyle for us all.

There is also a motivational *gift of ruling*, otherwise known as administrating or leading. There are those in the Body of Christ who manifest leadership and influence without much effort. For everyone else, this gift must be developed. The primary responsibility of governing is first personal: "He that is slow to anger is better than the mighty; and he that ruleth his spirit than he that taketh a city" (*KJV*, Prov. 16.32). We must have direction in our personal lives if we are to lead the Body of Christ. Fathers must administer their own households well before they show themselves able to rule to a greater extent (1 Tim. 3.4-5). The order of rule: rule yourself, your family, and then let Kingdom rule be an opportunity for the Holy Spirit to minister His love through you to those for whom you are responsible.

Romans chapter 12 lists the *gift of mercy* last. (Perhaps the last should be first.) We are able to learn a good deal about this gift in the parable of the Good Samaritan. After telling the parable, Jesus asked a lawyer which of the three who passed by had mercy on the wounded man. The lawyer rightly replied, "The one who showed pity and mercy to him" (Lk. 10.37a). Jesus responded, "Go and do likewise" (10.37b). Position yourself to practice mercy for "Blessed are the merciful, for they shall obtain mercy" (*KJV* Matt. 5.7).

BODY MINISTRY THROUGH THE GIFTS

Let us take a practical yet simple look at how the Romans' seven motivational gifts may be used within the body in the context of everyday living. Imagine a person very sick in a hospital bed. A group of Spirit-filled believers with differing gifts decides to visit this sick person. One in the group with the motivational gift of prophecy asserts, "What is God saying to us? Let us listen to His Spirit's voice."

The visitor with the gift of serving notices, "Your flowers are dying. Do you mind if I clean them up for you? First, let me adjust your bed for you. Are you comfortable?" This person was not thinking first about what God was speaking; she was thinking of the sick person's imminent needs. The server sees that the patient is uncomfortable and reaches out to help.

The teacher in the group offers, "There is something we can all learn from this suffering," as he gives a lesson to each of his "students."

This does not mean the teacher is unable to adjust the bed or that the server cannot hear God's voice. What this scenario reveals is that each person has a dominant motivational gift by which he or she quickly sees opportunities to use their gift.

. . . EACH PERSON HAS A DOMINANT MOTIVATIONAL GIFT BY WHICH HE OR SHE QUICKLY SEES OPPORTUNITIES TO USE THEIR GIFT.

The exhorter thinks aloud, "Wow! What we are doing here today is encouraging and caring." He or she then goes on to speak faith-building words to the patient. This person is anxious to share what happened in the hospital to the whole church. Everyone needs to be uplifted and cared for no matter what the situation.

The giver slips some money into the patient's hand as he says goodbye. He pulls his checkbook from inside his jacket and secretly pays some of the patient's bills.

The administrator pipes in, "I called your family earlier today to let them know that I have arranged meals to go to your home while you are in the hospital. I gave your wife a list of phone numbers from people who are willing to help."

"I can't tell you how much I hurt, and how sorry I am, at what's happening to you," sympathizes the person motivated by the gift of mercy, as he sits on the edge of the bed and gives the sick person a get-well card signed by friends and family.

Any ministry gifts a person has will function out of a motivational gift. For example, a person who is a servant by motivational gift could serve as a pastor who also prays for the sick. His ministry gifts of pastor and healing are motivated for service responsibilities. He has access to use whatever gifts are needed, as he serves the Body of Christ.

Although it is true that each believer has access to each gift, no single believer is able to function equally in all of the gifts. God has designed our limitations to require that we need each other. A pastor who tries to do everything may temporarily attempt to serve, prophesy, teach, exhort, give, and rule until a nervous breakdown results. God does not intend for all of the gifts to be flowing out of one person. Paul expands on this concept in 1 Corinthians 12, verses 14 through 27.

You may still be unaware of what gifts you have. You may know your manifestation ministry gift but not your motivational gift, or vice versa. Assess your own life, ask others, take a class on gifts, do an online gifts' assessment, discuss with your church elders, then respond to needs and exercise your gifts as you see opportunities. Discover and develop all of the gifts God has given you. Your gifts are included in this "so great salvation" which He purchased for you on Calvary and poured out on the day of Pentecost. Don't try to serve God with one hand tied behind your back by cords of unbelief. Break loose! Remember, you are free by divine decree! Be all He purposed for you to be! Go for it!

Part VI

The "Not guilty" are free to serve

Chapter 26
LOVE IS A FRUIT

The basis for Christian consecration is found in Romans 12.1-2. Humility and God-given gifts are the topics of Romans 12.3-8. Verses 9 through 13 admonish us to love all of our brothers and sisters in Christ, while verses 14 through 21 urge us to love all of mankind. This is a tall order for us who, before we were set free, lived a self-centered, sinful life. But now we must be taught to love as Christ loved. Not one of us has what it takes! Jesus Christ does have what it takes! As you and I focus on and draw from the roots of Romans chapters 4 through 8, we invite God to fill us with the fruit of His love in chapter 12. We will not have to force it because the root supplies life to the fruit, not the other way around. When we abide in the vine, fruit grows without struggle. Jesus teaches us to "abide in the vine" (*KJV*, Jn. 15).

LOVE FOR THE BRETHREN

"[Let your] love be sincere—a real thing" (Rom. 12.9a). The *New American Standard Bible* begins this same verse with, "Let love be without hypocrisy." This means not pretending we are someone we are not, but loving without phoniness. It is difficult, if not impossible, for the Holy Spirit to move through a person who is more interested in maintaining a façade than in loving others. As we yield to the Spirit's promptings, He will change us into His image. Protecting our self-made image is hard work. Jesus Christ did not die for our image; He died for the real you and me.

This hypocrisy is the opposite of sincerity, which means "without wax." The dishonest potters of Paul's day would often cover over their mistakes with wax to conceal the cracks in the pottery. When the buyer placed the vessel over a fire to cook, the wax melted and the liquid leaked out. The vessel was not fit for use. Pure love has no wax. Sincere love holds up under and withstands the fire.

JESUS CHRIST DID NOT DIE FOR OUR IMAGE; HE DIED FOR THE REAL YOU AND ME.

Honor one another: "hate what is evil (loathe all ungodliness, turn in horror from wickedness), but hold fast to that which is good. Love one another with brotherly affection—as members of one family—giving precedence *and* showing honor to one another" (9b-10). When we honor each other as brothers and sisters, we warmly respect each other. We are to love people and use things, not love things and use people. Men respect women, and women respect men. We are no longer squeezed into the world's mold. The Holy Spirit is able to renew and adjust our thinking. God tears down the old strongholds in our minds as we constantly yield ourselves to Him (Rom. 12.2).

"Rejoice *and* exult in hope; be steadfast and patient in suffering *and* tribulation; be constant in prayer" (12.12). Living a condemnation-free life frees us up to live rejoicing, hopeful, steadfast, patient, and prayerful lives. The encouragement of this verse should stir us to move on and mature in God whatever our past has been or our present surroundings are.

Finally, verse 13 begins by challenging us to show practical love for fellow believers: "Contribute to the needs of God's people—sharing in the necessities of the saints" and ends with a broader call to love, "pursuing the practice of hospitality." The *King James Version* translates the last part of verse 13 as "given to hospitality." This literally means that we are to love and welcome even strangers with the pure love of God.

FRUIT TAKES TIME

Love is a fruit of the Spirit. If we allow our roots to be planted and fed from the love of Christ revealed in chapters 4 through 8, love blossoms in and through us.

Concentrate on the root, not the fruit. The root grows best in the fertile soil of humility. Haughtiness will cause the root to shrivel up and die. When we recognize our own failures, we gain a whole new way of appreciating others.

CONCENTRATE ON THE ROOT, NOT THE FRUIT.

In God there is no instant fruit. People want patience, and they want it right now! Real fruit takes time to grow. There may be some instant visible changes in a person's life, but this is not yet mature fruit. It is impossible for any fruit to ripen overnight.

It is futile to try to hang articial fruit on your life. If in one day a recent convert looks as though he or she has a full-grown tree of fruit, be careful! The fruit may be made of wood, hay or stubble—or, worse yet, it may be plastic. Real fruit grows over time. The main difference between the gifts of the Spirit and the fruit of the Spirit is the gifts of the Spirit are complete when given but are developed by usage, whereas, the fruit of the Spirit starts from a seed and matures by abiding in Him (Jn. 15.4-5).

ZEAL

It is the power of the Spirit alone that changes us. That which is gained without the Spirit compromises the true zeal of God and gives the flesh an opportunity to take the credit. May you always have holy fire and passion, never lagging in zeal, full of the knowledge of God, aglow in the Spirit of God, in earnest endeavor serving the Lord!

LOVE TO ALL

Love your enemies. Not only are we called to participate in Christ's love for our fellow believers, but we are also called upon to bless and love our enemies. In Romans 12.14 through 15, the apostle urges us, through the inspiration of the Holy Spirit, to "Bless those who persecute you—who are cruel in their attitude toward you; bless and do not curse them. [Share others' joy], rejoicing with those who rejoice; and [share others' grief], weeping with those who weep." To the former defendants who are now set free, this is a totally new way of thinking and living.

Often it is more difficult to rejoice with those who rejoice than to weep with those who weep because another's rejoicing might be over something you have prayed for but they received. It is selfishness on our part that keeps us from rejoicing. We need to be changed, renewed in our thinking in order to rejoice with them. Rejoice! Do not "injure" their joy with your jealousy. And again, I say, Rejoice! Be happy!

"Live in harmony with one another; do not be haughty (snobbish, high-minded, exclusive)" (16a). If we find haughtiness and arrogance in our lives, we are not walking in the Spirit of Jesus Christ. Review and receive the life in chapters 4 through 8, die to self, and clean out judgmental exclusiveness. If you find yourself with a superior attitude of pride, "readily adjust yourself to [people, things] *and* give yourselves to humble tasks" (16b). How many of us choose humble tasks? Find a humble way to serve another person, and it will help them and deal with your pride. "Never overestimate yourself or be wise in your own conceits" (16b).

Don't be offensive! Show that you care when you "Repay no one evil for evil, but take thought for what is honest and proper and noble [aiming to be above reproach] in the sight of everyone" (17). In chapter 14 Paul elaborates on this subject of living so as not to offend someone else's fragile conscience, especially those of the household of faith. Factor in other people's feelings when you make your decisions.

"If possible, as far as it depends on you, live at peace with every one" (18). Everyone includes your spouse, your family, every brother and sister in Christ, unbelievers, and enemies. No one should purposely exclude others. Do not be a troublemaker; be a peacemaker. Live at peace with everyone and you will be blessed as a child of God (Matt. 5.9).

When others stir up trouble against you, do not try to avenge yourself, but rather, "leave the way open for [God's] wrath; for it is written, Vengeance is Mine, I will repay (requite), says the Lord" (19b). Do not get in God's way of settling issues. When we interrupt God's plan, we accomplish absolutely nothing. When God avenges, it is redemptive. Remember, Father knows best how to settle the score redemptively.

Bless and love everybody. This is not an abstract theory but a call to practical action. When we are really serious about spending our lives blessing and loving the way Jesus did, our goodwill will spread to even our enemies: "But if your enemy is hungry, feed him; if he is thirsty, give him drink; for by so doing you will heap burning coals upon his head. Do not be overcome by evil, but overcome (master) evil with good" (20-21). The Spirit grows all the nutritious fruit described in chapter 12 in the fertile, humble soil of Romans chapters 4 through 8.

While pioneering the church in Nairobi, I prayed that God would show me who would pastor the church when I left. Then during one Sunday evening service while I was praying for people at the altar, back in the pews I saw one man grab another man by the neck. I then saw my Kenya brother Samuel draw near to this conflict and shortly thereafter the two men involved were embracing each other. When I asked Samuel what the problem had been, he said one man owed the other money and could not pay it, so a fight was about to break out. Samuel reached into his pocket, paid the debt in full, and said: "Now you don't owe each other anything, so you two can be friends." That peacemaker spirit has kept Samuel as the pastor of All Nations Gospel Church and a leader in the Body of Christ for 45 years. I treasure his friendship.

The lifestyle of the defendants set free and walking in the challenges of everyday life calls for a humble attitude toward everyone, including our enemies. We will repay no man evil for evil, nor try to avenge ourselves. We will live at peace, spending our time feeding any hungry soul, including our enemies. We will not be overcome by the overwhelming evil around, but we will overcome evil with God's goodness. We will change our environment instead of letting the environment change us. In order to live such nobly free lives, we yield to the Spirit of God, allowing Him to prune and cut away branches that do not bring forth fruit. We will "be like a tree planted by the rivers of water, that brings forth fruit in its season, whose leaf also will not wither, and whatsoever he does shall prosper" (Psalm 1.3).

Chapter 27
SUBJECT TO GOVERNING AUTHORITIES

Romans chapter 13 contains even more fruit grown out of the roots of chapters 4 through 8. Since the defendants had lived their whole lives up to this time in rebellion toward God and society, they must see submission as the operative word in this new life of freedom. This chapter addresses the guidelines concerning submission, authority, and obedience to civil government. God is the source of all authority: "Let every person be loyally subject to the governing (civil) authorities. For there is no authority except from God—by His permission, His sanction; and those that exist do so by God's appointment" (1). No one occupies a position of authority except God allows it. He installs and removes authorities since He alone occupies the highest position of supreme authority. God has no peers!

PRINCIPLE OF SUBMISSION

Chapter 13 deals specifically with the principle of submission as it concerns believers and their civil government. This principle, however, operates on a grand scale throughout the Kingdom of God, as may be seen in all of Scripture. For instance, God ordains church apostles, prophets, evangelists, pastors, and teachers (Eph. 4.11). Although all believers have equal value, they do not all hold equal responsibilities in His Kingdom. We are provided plenty of opportunities to practice the principle of submission, whether it is to a pastor, a teacher, a parent, or the like. God distributes gifts as He wills (1 Cor. 12.11). Therefore, we must learn to submit to His sovereign decisions and appointments. Christ is the Head of His Body —the Church. Whenever someone attempts to usurp His headship, that person will eventually be cast aside. God will not grant His authority or leadership to those who grab it or usurp others' authority. Properly given authority must be guarded and not neglected. Authority grabbed is not genuine God-given authority but rather stolen authority. Authority is God-given to the man or woman who has accepted His assigned responsibilities.

Once a little boy said to his older brother, "Stop doing that!" The older brother retorted, "I don't have to listen to you." The younger one replied, "You must listen to me because mommy told me to tell you to stop." Authority was given to and used by the younger brother. Authority is authentic only when someone higher than the recipient gives it.

When we are in right relationship to God, we are not threatened by His authority. Rebellion is lifting up your head to the Lord in defiance. When we get to know Him, we identify with every aspect of His life, including the Cross. We follow Him in submission to His Father even to the point of rejection. We can trust such a loving leader Who submitted to His Father's will. He chose to die rather than to disobey His Father! The submission Jesus had before His Father was akin to the submission Isaac had to his father Abraham. Isaac submitted himself even if it meant death.

HE CHOSE TO DIE RATHER THAN TO DISOBEY HIS FATHER!

Submission is an attitude of the heart before it is an action. God desires us to submit to Him and not react to circumstances. The opposite of submission is rebellion. The attitude of submission is total. God places over us rightful authority for our own good. They may anger us when we do not possess a submitted attitude. God does not check with us to make sure we will like whatever our God-ordained authority has to say. God works His peace into our lives as we submit to proper human and spiritual authority. You can be sure that someone will come along to reveal pockets of rebellion and reaction still in us all!

Submitting to God is impossible when we do not know Jesus Christ. When we actively submit to God's will, we identify with Jesus Christ's death on the Cross.

SUBMISSION AND OBEDIENCE

We are not submitted to authority when we say, "I will submit here but not there." A consecrated life of submission produces a submissive lifestyle. The Lord will bless a submissive attitude and will empower us to obedient action. As Mary the Mother of Jesus commanded the servants at the wedding: "Whatever he says to you, do it" (Jn. 2.5b).

Someone might think, "What if some authority asks me to sin? Should I submit?" Never! We are never to go beyond the line the Scripture defines as sin. A submitted attitude can say, "I sure wish I could do what you ask, but if I did it would be sin. I would violate my conscience and I would not be submitted to God." In order to have healthy hearts, we must humbly submit to God and His authority.

Never compromise your conscience, "For whatever does not originate *and* proceed from faith is sin—that is, whatever is done without a conviction of its approval by God is sinful" (Rom. 14.23b). If you have no faith to do something, then do not do it. Do not choose to live in a faithless "fog." Meditate on, feed on, memorize, and study the written Word of God. A continuous feast on His Word will steadily bring your point of conscience closer and closer to what is Scripturally forbidden and what is not (see Ps. 119.9 and 11).

POINT OF CONSCIENCE

Our point of conscience was formed in part by the process of socialization in our family and society. As we mature in Christ,

6.24). Do not allow the devil to condemn you; rather allow Jesus to set you free from financial debt through Spirit-led disciplined budgeting. Live to please God. One easy preventative measure is to postpone a purchase until you have saved most of the full cost. By that time you may no longer need or even want it.

When my wife and I were first married, we had an opportunity to attend a "waterless cookware" demonstration in a friend's home. Thick aluminum pots and pans were used by the representative to cook up a wonderful meal shared by some of our friends. What could possibly be wrong with this scenario? At the end of the meal, a salesman came into the room and said, "Okay, it's time for the one-on-one sales pitch." He put pressure on us to buy and buy now. I had no peace. I told him, "No, we cannot buy these pots and pans now." At the time, we were pioneering a church in a needy area and had little money. We did have a few chipped porcelain pots.

The devil whispered into my spirit, "You've only got junk. You deserve something good for your wife. The people of God should have the best." At the time, the starter pot and pan set cost $133. It even had a lifetime warranty, but we would have gone into financial debt if we had purchased it. We walked out of that dinner without buying a thing. On the way home, my wife cried, and I felt horrible. All we could think about was the beautiful, shiny set of pots we could have had. Over time, the pots and pans didn't matter, but the practice of living debt-free served us well.

The following year, God called my wife and me as missionaries to Kenya. We packed the old chipped pots and prayed, "God, You will have to provide for us again." As we traveled around in preparation for going overseas, we visited a friend in Toledo, Ohio, who asked, "By the way, do you have pots and pans to take overseas?" We replied, "We only have chipped porcelain pots and pans."

Some time later, we returned to New York City to start packing for the Kenya move, when we received two large packages in the mail. To our surprise, every "waterless cookware" pot and pan was in the boxes. Unbeknown to us at the time, our friend in

Toledo was a salesman for the company. He contacted the other salesmen in the Toledo area and asked each one to give one pot or pan. We left for Africa with the entire set, not just the "starter set." We waited for God's timing without compromising our commitment to a debt-free lifestyle in order to be obedient to God's calling, and went to Kenya debt free!

If a person is willing to wait, God will not withhold any good thing from those who love Him and who walk uprightly (see Ps. 84.11). There is always a time gap between our need and God's supply. This is the faith gap. Do we have faith for what is not yet seen? If we presumptuously grasp for what we perceive we need by going into bad debt, we are not walking by faith in God. Our faith is exercised best in the time gap between when the need arises and when God supplies.

Sometimes, God will send an unexpected windfall of money to bless us. Never presume upon this option from God. He may choose to open the door for you to work a second job until you are debt-free. Either way, God is able to perform miracles to lead you out of debt if you choose and submit.

God has not called us to live our lives by waiting for miracles, but to live by His principles. Although God is able to work a miracle, He may choose, for His good purpose, to leave you in debt until you have learned godly spending principles. God our Heavenly Father does not raise spoiled children. He will not work an instant miracle every time you decide to buy impulsively.

It takes walking by the Spirit to insure that you will live with only one debt—the debt to love. You might wrongly think, "Well, if I just had more money, I would have no debts." The amount of money we have does not dictate whether or not we incur debts; neither does it guarantee happiness! Submission to the Holy Spirit will guide our financial well being. The last verse of Romans chapter 13 advises, "But clothe yourself with the Lord Jesus Christ, the Messiah, and make no provision for [indulging] the flesh—put a stop to thinking about the evil cravings of your physical nature—

to [gratify its] desires (lusts)" (14). The lusts of our physical natures are not just sensual or sexual; they are any "strong desires" our flesh has for the things of this world.

Do not be naïve. The enemy will try to put his thinking patterns into our minds. There are people who are unable to be in full-time ministry at home and abroad because they are so deeply in financial debt. Never owe your soul to anyone but the One Who died for you. You are eternally His, and His alone. According to verse 14, you and I must clothe ourselves with His robes of righteousness and make no provision for our flesh. Pray that God will enable you to receive this truth and live by His divine principles of economics.

Chapter 28
SCRUPLES

To enjoy the constant blessing of God in our lives, we must walk a disciplined, godly life in fellowship with other members of the Body of Christ. This means I do not make light of other people's convictions, and I do not let anyone talk me out of my convictions! Some Christians try to push their liberties on to other people. We have no legal right in Christ to force our freedoms on others. Chapter 14 of Romans teaches the truth that if my personal freedom violates the conviction of another, I am to forfeit my personal freedom for the sake of another. Always follow the Lord in love, according to your personal convictions.

When we become mature believers, we embrace even weak believers who have strict scruples. How we respond to weaker believers is a test of how well chapters 4 through 8 of Romans are at work in our lives. Are we going to push our beliefs onto others or, for their sakes, out of love, will we forego what we know is okay for a greater good—their spiritual growth in God?

You might think you have a great idea when you suggest, "Let's go bowling." Little do you know that a person with many scruples, including one against bowling, is in the room. He replies in a less-than-appreciative tone, "Bowling! That's ungodly. Jesus never bowled." This is only a test—a test of your love. What should you do? Try to find an alternative activity that suits everyone. You can bowl some other time.

Verse 1 commands us to welcome this kind of person into our group. No one will ever have a change of heart through an ugly attitude of exclusion or snobbery coming from a "believer." When we walk in God's love, the emphasis is on caring for one another.

you think His servant is out of line. Leave it to Him and watch how He changes the person's heart, if need be. Since the Father is merciful, long-suffering, and loving, He is able to make His servant "stand and be upheld, for the Master." He has His servants' best interest at heart, wanting them to mature and succeed.

Have you ever asked yourself, "How can they do that and call themselves Christians?" Always take it to the Father first in prayer. If He clears the way for you to speak directly to the "offender," go in a humble spirit to speak with your brother or sister about the issue. This is the Biblical pattern because "one man esteems one day as better than another, while another man esteems all days alike [sacred]. Let everyone be fully convinced (satisfied) in his own mind . . . None of us lives to himself (but to the Lord) . . ." (5-7). Then, if whatever they are doing is a direct violation of God's Word and they reject your counsel, take it to the proper church authority over them. Your motive will become clear. Do not be a Pharisee just looking for faults in others. Be like Jesus looking for someone to lift out of trouble. Jesus never whipped until He had first wept.

None of us lives to ourselves. Our moods, our ways, our business practices, our work or school functioning, all find their life, power and guidelines in the practice of chapters 4 through 8 of Romans. We are called to be like the One Who when He saw the prostitute being harassed by the Pharisees said, "Neither do I condemn you, go and sin no more" (Jn. 8.11).

"If we live, we live to the Lord, and if we die, we die to the Lord. So then, whether we live or we die, we belong to the Lord. For Christ died and lives again for this very purpose, that He might be Lord both of the dead and of the living" (8-9). We are to be thankful for both life and death because Jesus has conquered death and is alive forevermore!

In summary, re-evaluate your own attitude toward the believer with weaker faith and the one with stronger faith. This will help you become a mature follower of Jesus Christ. When you mature in love you will avoid offending others with your freedoms in order to protect the young ones both naturally and spiritually.

When you mature in love you abstain from judging another's servant concerning their freedoms. Any questionable practice by others that offends your conscience may be your opportunity to grow personally. Hold others up in prayer and, as the Holy Spirit leads, encourage or confront them gracefully.

2. LIVE IN THE LIGHT OF THE JUDGMENT SEAT OF GOD

A second measure of maturity is found in verse 10: "Why do your criticize *and* pass judgment on your brother . . . For we shall all stand before the judgment seat of God." Ultimately, each one of us will give an account of himself or herself to God. It is the work of the Holy Spirit to bring to light those things in us that need to be changed.

WHATEVER WE DO IN THIS LIFE WILL RECEIVE ITS FINAL REWARD ON THE LEVEL OF OUR MOTIVES.

It is before the *Bema* judgment seat of God where Christians will witness their works of wood, hay, and stubble burn up (1 Cor. 3.12-15). This is not a judgment for sin, but a standard for rewards. All we did for selfish purposes has already received its earthly reward. We, the redeemed, will be in heaven, but the works we did on earth for ourselves, to be seen by men, will have no eternal reward. It is before the judgment seat of God that the secret works of obedience will be openly rewarded. "And so each of us shall give an account of himself to God" (Rom. 14.12). Whatever we do in this life will receive its final reward on the level of our motives.

Want to measure your maturity in Christ? Count how many decisions you make in light of the judgment seat of God. Live in the light of eternity and your ministry will be a "labor of love" with eternal dividends.

3. WALK IN LOVE

The third measure of maturity is actually walking in love. Do you cause undue hurt and injury to your fellow believers? Open up to Christ's love because " . . . if your brother is being pained *or* his feelings hurt *or* if he is being injured by what you eat, [then] you are no longer walking in love.—That is, you have ceased to be living and conducting yourself by the standard of love toward him . . ." (15). A mature person aims not to offend others or to become easily offended. A mature person is able to handle each situation in a redemptive way. Jesus reduced all the law to two commandments: "Love your God . . . Love your neighbor" (Matt. 22.37-39).

A pastor friend of mine who lives in Harlem, New York, once prayed for a woman to be delivered from drunkenness. The following service she came more drunk than ever. One night at 2 a.m. she called the pastor from a local bar and said: "Pastor, I have drunk more than what I can pay for and have told the bartender that you will come and pay." As soon as she hung up, the pastor and his wife went to the bar. They saw her slumped over. They paid the bill and took her home with them. After that she drank no more. When the pastor asked her how she was delivered, she said, "When I knew you loved me even when I was drunk, I didn't need to drink any more."

Christ enables us to walk in love and embrace our weaker brother or sister. We are empowered not to live for ourselves but for His service. "For it is written, As I live, says the Lord, every knee shall bow to Me, and every tongue shall confess to God—that is, acknowledge Him to His honor and to His praise" (Rom. 14.11). The Lordship of Christ must reign supreme over every detail of our lives.

4. LIVE IN LIGHT OF CALVARY

"Do not let what you eat hurt *or* cause the ruin of one for whom Christ died" (15b). The fourth measure of maturity is to live in light of Calvary. A mature believer does not criticize because they know Christ died for everyone, the weak and the strong, the poor and the rich, the mature and immature "for God so loved the world" (Jn. 3.16). Keep Calvary always clear in your sight. The Cross gives value to every person. He forever assigned equal worth to all humans by His death on the Cross.

Does this high value, then, mean you and I are free to do whatever we want to do? No, that would only tend to compromise our worth. Jesus freed us from the wrath of God to know His love and submit to His way. Submission is a love response. Sometimes His way brings you and me in touch with "narrow-minded" people. It is your assignment to care for them. Christ cared enough to die for us; therefore, we should recognize each person as extremely valuable and protect his or her dignity.

SUBMISSION IS A LOVE RESPONSE!

"The Kingdom of God is not a matter of [getting the] food and drink [one likes]" (17a). The Kingdom of God is about better things: "but instead, it is righteousness—that state which makes a person acceptable to God—and heart-peace and joy in the Holy Spirit" (17b). This is the kingdom order: righteousness first, peace as the fruit of righteousness, and joy the result. Real joy cannot be experienced without righteousness—right standing with God.

5. LIVE ACCEPTABLE TO GOD AND APPROVED BY MAN

Verse 18 holds the fifth measure of maturity: "He who serves Christ in this way is acceptable *and* pleasing to God and is approved by men." Are you pleasing God with your life? Do you sense the approval of people because they feel your love? As we live in obedience to what God tells us, and within the common standards of decency among men and women in our culture, we are acceptable to God and approved by men. Notice, "acceptable to God" comes before "approved by men!"

6. LIVE IN THE ATTITUDE OF HARMONY AND MUTUAL EDIFICATION

"So let us then definitely aim for *and* eagerly pursue what makes for harmony and for mutual upbuilding (edification and development) of one another" (19). God does not give gifts of "divisiveness" or "fruit inspecting" to anyone. In the church, at home, and at work, some people are critical and divisive. Instead of playing one harmonious chord in God's great symphony, this type of person strikes discordant notes of division, disharmony, and confusion.

Whenever a truly mature set-free believer is placed in a situation with fighting factions, in time peace prevails. Jesus Christ always brings true peace. The Beatitudes say, "Blessed *are* the peacemakers" (*KJV*, Matt. 5.9a) and the next verse says, "Blessed are they which are persecuted for righteousness' sake . . . (*KJV*, Matt. 5.10a). Peacemaking and persecution go hand-in-hand. When you become a peacemaker, the fighting parties may turn their anger on you. The Cross of Christ is both the place of peace and the place of great persecution. Jesus absorbed our persecution and gave us His peace at the Cross.

"It is a good thing to remember and a better thing to do, to work with the construction gang than with the wrecking crew." You and I have been commissioned to be a part of constructing and re-constructing the precious lives of people. We aim for constructiveness, peace, and harmony. Be vigilant to stay on the construction team. Disharmony is not the work of God; it is the work of the accuser/deceiver.

The sixth measure of a mature believer is the ability to lift up fallen people and to make them feel like the valuable persons they really are. Our job is to keep the peace and restore: "Ye that are spiritual restore . . ." (Gal. 6.1).

7. LIVE IN THE LIGHT OF YOUR CONVICTIONS AND FAITH

The seventh measure of maturity is the ability to keep one's personal convictions to oneself: "Your personal convictions [on such matters] exercise as in God's presence, keeping them to yourself—striving only to know the truth and obey His will" (Rom. 14.22a). What kinds of matters are we to keep to ourselves? Personal matters like food, drink, special days, and customs that believers may not see eye to eye on. If you witness someone else doing what you do not feel free to do, do not judge. I am not talking about the essential core beliefs of Christianity. If we are truly a part of the mature Body of Christ, we must be willing to allow for differences. For example, two boys live in a family. One boy is twelve years old and the other five. When the mother commands the five year old to go to bed at 8 o'clock, he tries to get her to treat him as his older brother who is twelve and is allowed to stay up two hours longer. Different levels of maturity require different guidelines in line with personal spiritual development. Since when has God called us to be so conformed to each other that we must all have the same personal convictions? We are to be conformed to His standard, which is Jesus and His Word. Personal convictions are not uniform nor do they have to be. Release others to follow the personal promptings of the Holy Spirit. In Romans chapters 4 through 8, we learned we have been buried with Christ. If we are dead with Him then minor personal convictions will not divide us.

Chapter 14 admonishes us not to go laying our personal convictions on everybody else. Keep them to yourself instead. "A [self-confident] fool has no delight in understanding, but only in revealing his personal opinions *and* himself" (Prov. 18.2). There may be certain "divine limitations" God has put on you. As you obey His specific instructions, the Spirit will increase your spiritual growth and life.

"Blessed, happy, to be envied is he who has no reason to judge himself for what he approves—who does not convict himself by what he chooses to do" (Rom. 14.22b). You and I know people who are truly happy because they are doing what they enjoy. They avoid violating their convictions. This person is truly free to serve God and free to worship Him without distractions.

"But the man who has doubts—misgivings, an uneasy conscience—about eating, and then eats [perhaps because of you], stands condemned [before God], because he is not true to his convictions *and* he does not act from faith" (23a). You might be tempted to persuade him to try just a small drink and then you proceed to put some questionable drink in his glass. He drinks. Even though he has an uneasy conscience, you have convinced him to listen to you, rather than his conscience. Now he "stands condemned." He is no longer free because He did not respond to the personal convicting power of the Holy Spirit, but to your overpowering influence. God is not the One condemning him because it has already been established that "There is therefore now no condemnation to them who are in Christ Jesus" (*KJV*, Rom. 8.1a). The one who violates his own conscience condemns himself. He now can be freed only by confessing, "Father, forgive me. I receive Your life and repent." The mature believer will never put another person in a compromising position. These guidelines may include things like movies, attire, sports, drink, amusements, relationships/associations, and conduct.

Whenever certain people pressure others, the weaker ones are unable to respond in faith because their consciences have been injured. For them it is sin! "For whatever does not originate and proceed from faith is sin—that is, whatever is done without a conviction of its approval by God is sinful" (14.23b). Can it be any clearer? Whatever does not originate in faith, cannot be done in faith. If you do not feel free in your conscience to do something, it is not for you at this time. When something is not clear to you, avoid it. If in doubt, leave it out! Move only in faith, because as you mature your conscience will line up more with the Holy Scripture.

ROBUST FAITH

The apostle turns his remarks to a specific group at the start of the next chapter: "We who are strong [in our convictions and of robust faith]" (Rom.15.1a). Robust faith is a very rugged kind of faith. It is the kind of faith that when knocked down rebounds stronger. This faith gives the right balance to life and enables steady forward progress.

Circumstances may come into your life that may cause you to have misgivings, but be encouraged again because of your robust faith in Jesus. When critics judge you or your gift, do not give up. How sad it is when a believer is hurt and offended by another brother's or sister's critical words! Robust faith has the ability to forgive the offender and to rise above the hurt in Jesus' name.

When we have robust faith, we "ought to help carry the doubts and qualms of others—and not to please ourselves" (1b). A person of robust faith is able to help not only himself, but others who have periods of doubt and pangs of conscience. The example set before us by Paul is none other than Jesus Christ Who ". . . (gave no thought to His own interests) to please Himself . . ." (15.3). "Go and do likewise" (Lk. 10.28).

Chapter 29
EVANGELISM AND MISSIONS

The theme of Romans chapter 15 is evangelism and missions. Salvation always matures to the point of loving and reaching out to others with the knowledge of Jesus Christ.

CROSSES YOUR WILL

If this chapter were located in the early part of this book, we may not have been able to understand it. We need the truths of chapter 4 through 8 of Romans especially to be able to respond to this chapter. This chapter is not about us; when His will is revealed our wills must yield. This subject of missions crosses our wills. We have not been released from God's courtroom in order to go out and "please ourselves" (see 15.1-3). All of us are called to grow into mature Christians who will submit their times and desires to Him as our "reasonable service." Since missions is always on God's heart, a mature believer's heart beats in harmony with His. Our life's mission is His Great final Commission—"Go into all the world!"

OUR LIFE'S MISSION IS HIS GREAT FINAL COMMISSION—GO INTO ALL THE WORLD!

When we engage in evangelism, we focus on God's burden and concern. Jesus Christ did not live to please Himself; He lived to please His Father. We are born again not to live for our own pleasure, but for the pleasure of the One who died for us.

"Now may the God Who gives the power of patient endurance

(steadfastness) and Who supplies encouragement, grant you to live in such mutual harmony *and* such full sympathy with one another, in accord with Christ Jesus . . . Welcome *and* receive (to your hearts) one another, then, even as Christ has welcomed *and* received you, for the glory of God" (Rom. 15.5-7). These verses address how strong believers can strengthen and unify the Body of Christ as spiritual parents to reach out and embrace those who are just starting the Christian life. Good parents kneel down to eye level with each child. This is exactly what our Heavenly Father did for us. He sent His Son Jesus in human form to stoop down to our eye level and lift us up to His.

TO THE GENTILES

Romans 15.9 through 12 explains the reasons for Christ's mission to the Gentiles:

> ". . . That the Gentiles might glorify God for His mercy; as it is written, 'For this cause I will confess to Thee among the Gentiles, and sing unto Thy name.' And again He saith, 'Rejoice ye Gentiles, with His people.' And again, 'Praise the Lord, all ye Gentiles; and laud Him, all ye people.' And again, Isaiah saith, 'There shall be a root of Jesse, and He that shall rise to reign over the Gentiles; in Him shall the Gentiles trust.'" (*KJV*)

Christ includes the Gentiles because He knows they too will praise Him and receive His salvation. The second Psalm confirms this fact: ". . . Ask of Me, and I will give You the nations as Your inheritance, and the uttermost parts of the earth for Your possession . . ." (Ps. 2.8).

Gentiles is another word for "nations" and "peoples." God wants to give us our inheritance from the nations. In prayer and intercession, He gives us power to dispel the darkness and claim our inheritance. In verses 9 through 12 of chapter 15, the word

Gentiles is used some 11 times. This emphasizes the theme of this chapter is that the Gentiles might know Him—God's mission statement. Believing Jews and believing Gentiles together will worship the true and living God.

The teaching in Romans is progressively worked in us to properly prepare us to function within the Body of Christ. Obedience to the Great Commission that "the Gentiles might glorify God" (9) is our individual and corporate calling. This is the culmination of the whole book of Romans. Nothing tests our maturity more than our attitudes and actions toward the lost. A fruit of mature believers is their commitment to reach across the street or around the world to "win for the Lamb the reward of His suffering" *(Moravian motto).*

THERE IS NOTHING THAT TESTS OUR MATURITY MORE THAN OUR ATTITUDES AND ACTIONS TOWARD THE LOST.

OUR RESPONSIBILITY

How do we recognize a bad attitude toward the needy? Jesus answered this question in Luke 10.29-39. Some religious men, wrapping their robes around themselves, passed right by a beaten man. However, the Good Samaritan demonstrated "pity *and* mercy to him." He ministered to him in his hour of need. Compassion is love in action. A self-centered attitude is not compatible with what Christ did for us. How can we keep such Good News to ourselves when so many have never heard of salvation through Jesus Christ?

COMPASSION IS LOVE IN ACTION!

Paul, under the inspiration of the Holy Spirit, personally takes the responsibility to let the Gentiles know: ". . . so that through me the (Gospel) message might be fully proclaimed and all the Gentiles might hear it . . ." (2 Tim. 4.17). He modeled for all of us what we have been commissioned to do (see Matt. 28.19-20).

The message of Romans frees us from bondage, then empowers us with boldness to take the Gospel across the street and to the uttermost parts of the earth, that nations might know the praises of God. You and I are responsible! Someone might argue, "I am free! I did not bargain for this; I prefer His blessings only." We are safer with the breakings of God than with the blessings of God. When God breaks us, there is humility and the release of His Spirit. The combination of His blessings and breakings produces spiritual balance.

WE ARE SAFER WITH THE BREAKINGS OF GOD THAN WITH THE BLESSINGS OF GOD.

UNITY

We are all to be of one mind: "That together you may (unanimously) with united hearts *and* one voice, praise and glorify the God and Father of our Lord Jesus Christ, the Messiah" (6). We are free to live in the unity of the Spirit, with a single-hearted purpose. We find this concept of unity only this once in Romans, but many times in the book of Acts. The unity established in the book of Acts spurred on great church growth and expansion. When disunity comes into a church, it compromises the spirit of evangelism and missions. Whenever a church is divided, its missionary vision is in jeopardy. If the enemy traps us into division, then our foe has undermined our ability to fulfill the Great Commission. Put aside your fickle excuses and differences, lest they hinder the extension of the Gospel! It takes a people of "one heart and one mind" to extend the Gospel worldwide.

BY THE POWER OF THE HOLY SPIRIT

In making his final appeal to the strong of faith, Paul encourages us with these words: "[And as my preaching has been accompanied] with the power of signs and wonders, [and all of it] by the power of the Holy Spirit. So that starting from Jerusalem and as far round as Illyricum I have fully preached the Gospel . . . (19). May God release through our lives a new dimension and dynamic of the Holy Spirit to see signs and wonders in these last days. The world needs more than communication; it needs to see a demonstration of what we believe and preach. Paul said it was the Holy Ghost power that enabled him and will empower us to believe for signs and wonders. We do not have sufficient power in and of ourselves. Yield to and embrace what the Spirit wants to do through you for Jesus promised we would do even greater things (see Jn. 14.12). Remember, God's greatest sign has come in the form of a baby born of a Virgin, conceived by the Holy Spirit, and raised in obscurity. Some people missed that wonderful sign because there was no room in the inn (Lk. 2.7b). Not much has changed in 2000 years!

THE WORLD NEEDS MORE THAN COMMUNICATION; IT NEEDS TO SEE A DEMONSTRATION OF WHAT WE BELIEVE AND PREACH.

No one can rightfully say, "I don't have a signs and wonders ministry." Jesus promised: ". . . these signs will accompany those who believe . . ." (Mk.16.17a). True signs and wonders are so authentic that our enemy may perform counterfeits in order to try to deceive (see 2 Thess. 2.9). Counterfeit money is evidence the real thing exists. Those who believe need only yield to the Spirit, and as they go signs and wonders will surely follow—it's His promise.

The apostle Paul never looked for the path of least resistance in his missionary travels. He followed wherever Christ led: "Thus my ambition has been to preach the Gospel, not where Christ's name has already been known, lest I build on another man's foundation; But [instead I would act on the principle], as it is written, They shall see who have never been told of Him, and they shall understand who have never heard [of Him]" (Rom. 15. 20-21). What a novel idea! Go somewhere where there is no competition with the next church or mission. Go somewhere where your dedicated life will light the darkness of a village, a city, or a nation. Paul's goal was to establish churches where no man had ever preached. Those places still exist today! Maybe next door?

Paul not only established churches where no one else had gone; he also cared for the churches that needed help:

> . . . since I have longed for enough years to come to you, I hope to see you in passing [through Rome] as I go [on my intended trip] to Spain, and to be aided on my journey there by you after I have enjoyed your company for a little while. For the present, however, I am going to Jerusalem to bring aid (relief) for the saints—God's people there. For it has been the good pleasure of Macedonia and Achaia to make some contribution for the poor among the saints of Jerusalem. (15.23-26)

He has passed the torch to every following generation who will carry it to regions beyond. It is no longer acceptable for you and me to hear the Gospel over and over when millions have never heard it once. ". . . Go ye into all the world and preach and publish openly the good news . . ." (Mk. 16.15). The harvest is ripe; the laborers are few!

PART VII

FAREWELL

Chapter 30
SAFEGUARDS

Chapter 15 of Romans begins the book's final countdown. Chapter 16 provides a "fence of protection" for the believer. The defendants have been set free to live the Christian life wherever God places them. They need to recognize two very important protective boundaries.

After giving greetings in the first half of chapter 16, Paul begins to emphasize the first boundary: "I appeal to you, brethren, to be on your guard concerning those who create dissensions and difficulties *and* cause division, in opposition to the doctrine—the teaching —which you have been taught. [I warn you to turn aside from them, to] avoid them" (17). The first safeguard is to stay clear from people who create dissension and division. Keep a watchful eye on those who try to drive a wedge between you and your leaders! The separation God requires is between believers and troublemakers, not between believers, their leaders, elders, and brothers and sisters.

KEEP A WATCHFUL EYE ON THOSE WHO TRY TO DRIVE A WEDGE BETWEEN YOU AND YOUR LEADERS!

Beware of someone with a disloyal and divisive spirit. It does not make any difference which church these people go to, they will find a reason to disagree and be divisive. This type of person may approach an unsuspecting member of the church and offer to give them a personal, private "word from God." If he or she is not submitted to the proper leadership, discord is being sown. If undetected, the divisive one can undermine the church leadership.

When the troublemaker has accomplished his or her purpose, the innocent listener is not so innocent any more and may have been detoured from sound teaching and healthy Christian fellowship in the Lord.

The closer we get to Jesus, the closer we get to each other! The book of Romans makes this clear. As you and I behold Him, the One the whole book is about, the Holy Spirit changes us into His image. King David recognized this truth when he wrote, "As for me, I will behold thy face in righteousness: I shall be satisfied, when I awake, with thy likeness" (*KJV*, Ps. 17.15).

AVOID FLATTERY

A second safeguard is located in verse 18: "For such persons do not serve our Lord Christ but their own appetites *and* base desires, and by ingratiating and flattering speech they beguile the hearts of the unsuspecting and simple-minded [people]." The enemy's strategy is to puff up people, appealing to their pride, to think they are more spiritual than others. Believers walk in the supernatural not the super spiritual. Recognize those persons who come with flattering speech and smooth words to sweet-talk you back into base desires and condemnation. Paul began his letter to the Galatians by warning them of "another Gospel" (Gal. 1.6). Stand with your church leaders and elders. God has placed these two protections around our lives to guard us from attack and to protect the Body for which He died, so avoid troublemakers and flatterers.

Big-selling gossip magazines are on every newsstand because people want to know something "juicy" about the private lives of others. There is a tremendous carnal desire to know who is divorced and much more than a little personal information. This same divisive chatter plagues the church. Paul is saying that people who stir up division or who sweet-talk other believers with flattery are separating believers from both sound teaching and their beloved brethren and leaders.

What, then, should one do if a problem is identified within a local church? First, do not cause division or you may be the source of a more severe problem. Second, pray for the offender to humble himself or herself in order for God to work. Remember from chapter 14, if we have a problem with one of God's servants we are to go first to their Master. We can tell Him and trust that He has it all under control. Third, God may or may not direct you to speak with the one who has the problem. After much prayer and church counsel, you and possibly an elder would then go with a redemptive attitude.

Keep in mind the new fruit of freedom takes time to ripen. Concentrate on establishing the healthy roots of Romans chapters 4 through 8. If, after time, you do not see any fruit in your life, return to the root. Take time to focus on the work Jesus Christ has done for you. It is not about what you are doing for Him as much as the fact that He has already provided full sweet victory for you. Return to the courtoom argument which set you free and renew your faith.

RELATIONSHIPS "IN THE LORD"

Whereas the first two boundaries of protection (beware and avoid) are negative, Paul adds a third, which is positive: the need for Christian relationships. He now takes time to acknowledge and give thanks for the relationships with those whom he has worked so closely. Tertius, Paul's fellow laborer, whose hand wrote this Epistle, sends his own personal greeting (Rom. 16.22). Paul goes on to greet at least twenty-six additional people by name as well as several home-based churches. In addition, he sends greetings from nine saints who were with him at the time. Notice the recognition he gives to a number of women who ministered in the Gospel, especially Phoebe, who most likely carried his letter to the saints in Rome and is to be received "in the Lord" (16.2a).

Paul repeats these words "in the Lord" over and over in chapter 16. There is a new perception and appreciation for one another when we are "in the Lord." We are able to say, "I receive you, my sister, in the Lord" and "I receive you, my brother, in the Lord." Paul continues, "Remember me to Ampliatus, my beloved in the Lord" (8) and "Salute those workers in the Lord . . . who have worked so hard in the Lord" (12). Paul remembered the names of the godly workers "in the Lord" through a long list of personal greetings.

The one thing that Paul was determined to know about his fellow believers was "to be conscious of [nothing]—among you except Jesus Christ, the Messiah, and Him crucified" (1 Cor. 2.2b). He wanted to know the Head better by knowing the members of His body. Paul modeled for us this new and deep relationship among people who are "in the Lord."

Chapter 31
FAITH POWERS US FORWARD

Take another look at the big picture painted throughout the book of Romans by returning to chapter 1 verse 8: "First, I thank my God through Jesus Christ for you all, that your faith is spoken of throughout the whole world" (*KJV*). At the start, Paul called the readers' attention to their great faith! He completes the big picture view in verse 19 of chapter 16 when he writes: "For your obedience is come abroad unto all *men*" (*KJV*). Robust faith leads to obedient worldwide action. Why? Obedience is the fruit of faith (Rom. 1.5). Obedience gets the job done.

ROBUST FAITH LEADS TO OBEDIENT WORLDWIDE ACTION.

OBEDIENCE OF FAITH

People around the world were not only hearing of the believers' faith; they saw evidence of their obedience as well. "For your obedience is come abroad unto all *men*" (*KJV*, 16.19). From the first chapter to the last, the book of Romans puts beautiful feet on the mountains of fulfillment. The book's final analysis comes in the next-to-last verse: "But now is made manifest, and by the scriptures of the prophets, according to the commandment of the everlasting God, made known to all nations for the obedience of faith" (*KJV*, 26). What has been made known to all nations? According to the *Amplified Bible*, the "obedience to the faith" which "is made known to all nations."

God wants to change our world for the better. Where there is doubt, He wants to give His faith. The robust faith that He gives produces the ability to walk this Christian life in obedience. What the world sees is our obedient behavior—the fruit of our faith.

LOOKING FOR A PLACE TO LAND

Looking back over the past 2000 years, one can see the Divine strategy of a loving God revealed in His great plan of salvation. The letter to the Romans is a road map to chart the course for us today.

As Paul closes this exquisite thesis on God's plan for mankind, he begins as a pilot to circle the airplane looking for a good landing place. In chapter 15.33 he gives his first indication of landing when he says, "May (our) peace-giving God be with you all! Amen—so be it. " In Romans 16.20 he puts down the landing gear with "and the God of peace will soon crush Satan under your feet. The grace of our Lord Jesus Christ, the Messiah, be with you." He circles for his approach again in Romans 16.24: "The grace of our Lord Jesus Christ, the Messiah, be with you all. Amen—so be it."

RECEIVING STRENGTH FOR THE JOURNEY AHEAD

Finally, a signal from the tower gives him full clearance to land the Romans plane in verses 25 to 27. As we see the landing field approaching, we scan the countryside and remember that we taxied out from a state of **human condemnation** in chapters 1 to 3 and took off from the runway of chapters 4 and 5, where faith caught the wind of **complete justification**. The flight continued through some turbulence in chapters 6 and 7 and soared on into beautiful clouds of **continuous sanctification**. Paul then landed in a new place of **divine vindication** by the Spirit in chapter 8, stepping out and enjoying a new life of **practical consecration** (chapters 12-16).

Do you desire more faith? Reach back into chapter 4. Do you want more victory? Identify again with Christ in chapters 5 and 6. Throw off bondages of the Law in chapter 7. Embrace the Holy Spirit who is able to defy the law that pulls you down. In chapter 8 "there is now no condemnation" because you are free. You have been released from the weight of sin and from the condemnation of the Law. Enjoy your "new marriage" and produce fruit. Walk in the blessed truth of chapter 8, as it is your bill of rights guaranteeing that whatever you need, He has already done for you. Accept the challenge to proclaim the "good news" of the Gospel for it is God's power working unto salvation to everyone who believes. The same power of the Holy Spirit will make alive to you every word of this beloved book of Romans.

The final farewell and touchdown is made in chapter 16 verses 25 through 27:

> Now to Him that is of power to stablish you according to my gospel, and the preaching of Jesus Christ, according to the revelation of the mystery, which was kept secret since the world began, but now is made manifest, and by the Scriptures of the prophets, according to the commandment of the everlasting God, made known to all nations for the obedience of faith: To God only wise, be glory through Jesus Christ forever. Amen." (*KJV*)

Oh, the grace that reached down and took us from our lost, hopeless condition where we were under condemnation from the devilish prosecutor who, using the Law, had built his airtight case against us. It was the introduction of unexpected evidence that determined our judgment would not be according to Law, but by grace. The One who stood with nail-scarred hands reaching out to all presented Himself as the new evidence. He turned the case around and where there was despair, He gave us hope. Where there was death, He now gives life. Our Defender stayed on the case until He saw you and me walk out of the courtroom and into the sunlight of His love—free at last. Even today, He sits at the right hand of God the Father as our Defense "actually pleading as He intercedes for us" (Rom. 8.34b). "All our praise is focused through Jesus on the incomparable wise God" *(The Message)*. He is always loving us and will never leave us. May we in turn, who have received so much, be eternally grateful by bowing our knees in obedience to His command to have faith and take action. Amen!

Appendix 1
PURPOSE AND HISTORY

A DIVINE LIMITATION

Due to the travel limitations in the author's day, today we are able to enjoy a wealth of knowledge and revelation written down in the book of Romans. The apostle wrote to his audience, "For I am yearning to see you" (Rom. 1.11a). Paul had heard that the Gospel had crossed over the many hazardous mountains and a sea to Greece, Macedonia, and then to Rome. The Holy Spirit knew that if Paul had gone to Rome when he wanted, he would have taught only the Roman believers of his day. The record would not then be with us today. So there came upon Paul's life travel restrictions. He had this desire to see God's people in Rome, thus he wrote to them.

OUR DISAPPOINTMENTS ARE GOD'S APPOINTMENTS!

According to history, Paul eventually did travel to Rome where he was beheaded. The fact is, however, he was not at first able to do what he prayed to do, desired to do, and planned to do. His travel restriction provided for you and me the blessing of his letter to the Romans, a letter that we otherwise would not have had. Our disappointments are God's appointments!

It is not dos and don'ts that change us; rather it is the Holy Spirit's conviction and power that changes us. Remember, Romans was written because Paul had a desire to go to Rome, but could not get there at first. The fact that Paul was repeatedly frustrated in that goal is the avenue for revelation in his writings.

When God frustrates our plans it is because He has a far deeper, far more eternal weight of purpose He wants to work out. You might say, "Oh, God, I have wanted to go there so many times, but you will not let me." It is because He has something else in mind for you, something you cannot see. Paul's frustration in getting to Rome worked out for the good of ALL of us.

The book of Romans deals with our pride because it reveals the salvation found in Christ alone. Therefore, we have no room for pride. When we complete this study of Romans, we will not have a self-righteous leg left on which to stand. No defense! There is no deed you or I have ever done or can do that we will be able to point to and say, "Because of this, or because of that I am saved." None of our deeds has any merit with respect to our salvation. Thus, our pride takes a deathblow. If you had said or thought, "Well, I'm glad I am not as bad as those people," you will not be able to think that anymore for "All have sinned and come short of the glory of God" (*NKJV*, Rom. 3.23).

ROMANS IN HISTORY

There are nine letters written by Paul to churches: Romans, 1 & 2 Corinthians, Galatians, Ephesians, Philippians, Colossians, and 1 & 2 Thessalonians. Four Pauline letters are written to individuals: 1 & 2 Timothy, Titus, and Philemon.

FOUNDATIONAL IN BIBLE ORDER

Although one of the first books written by Paul was to the church in Rome, it was written on his third missionary journey and has been sandwiched between Acts and First Corinthians in New Testament order.

Romans is the establishing, foundational book which contains many solid truths. The truth that justification is by faith means we are declared righteous. This truth is repeated again in Corinthians and Galatians when Paul deals with correcting the false doctrines that were present in those churches.

To more fully understand the revelation of our legal freedom in Christ, study Romans' sister book, Galatians. The freedom presented in Romans is expounded on in Galatians. For example, Galatians confronts the erroneous teaching that a person may be saved by works. Galatians 1.6 states, "I am surprised *and* astonished that you are so quickly turning renegade *and* deserting Him Who invited *and* called you by the grace (unmerited favor) of Christ, the Messiah, [and that you are transferring your allegiance] to a different, *even* an opposition gospel." This is a grave mistake. The Spirit saves us; we must appropriate it by faith. We live by the same power by which we were saved. Paul explains that we do not get saved by the Spirit and then work our salvation out living by the flesh. He affirms that all of salvation comes by the Spirit. The Spirit makes us righteous, and we are kept righteous by the same Spirit, not by works that we do.

Romans first presents foundational truths, then Paul's other letters elaborate for emphasis. Corinthians also expounds on one of Romans' foundational teachings: spiritual gifts in the church. Paul establishes in Romans that we have been made dead to sin and resurrected to life with Christ. In Ephesians Paul further explains our position as we are seated with Christ. Finally, in 1 Thessalonians 4.17, he asserts that we are awaiting the return of Christ, to be caught up to meet Him in the air. Paul affirms our position in Christ continuously in each of his letters.

TIME AND PLACE WRITTEN

When, then, was Romans written? Some say that it was written in 55 AD, while others say 56 or 57 AD, and still others believe that it was written in the spring of 58 AD. It is not necessary to quibble over the exact year, but I personally believe that the book was written at the latest date in the spring of 58 AD. From Acts 20.3 we learn that Paul was in Corinth where it is believed he wrote the book of Romans. From the first chapter of Romans we know that he still had not traveled to Rome. He knew his time was running out. He finally did make it to Rome, but not as he had expected. Paul hoped to go to Rome as a preacher, instead he went as a prisoner.

Paul's letter to the Romans made it to those saints before he did, most likely via a faithful Christian sister named Phoebe. It is easy for us in the twenty-first century, western culture to accept Paul's feminine letter carrier. In the eastern culture 2000 years ago, however, such a vital ministry for a woman may have been unacceptable. In Romans we recognize that females were not undervalued in the early church. Paul certainly trusted this Christian sister. She was an important part of the church family and useful in the Body of Christ.

ROMANS IS THE GRAND DYNAMIC OF TRUE CHRISTIANITY, AS IT INCLUDES FIRST BELIEVING, THEN DOING.

Paul had help writing his book (Rom. 16.22). Although dictated by Paul, Romans was penned by Tertius. In Romans chapter 16, verse 23, we see that Gaius hosted Paul as he and Tertius worked on this important foundational letter. The book of Romans was written originally to a church that was in real need of a clearly defined salvation message. It was written also to all future generations who also have need of the same clearly outlined message.

REPRESENTATIVE COMMENTARIES

Martin Luther's opinion concerning Romans is found in the preface to his *Commentary on Romans:* "This Epistle is really the chief part of the New Testament and the very purest Gospel, and is worthy not only that every Christian should know it word for word, by heart, but occupy himself with it every day, as the daily bread of the soul. It can never be read or pondered too much, and the more it is dealt with the more precious it becomes, and the better it tastes" (xiii). Let your soul constantly run through the pages and pick up the truths. Allow your mind to exercise memorization of each of its words. *Matthew Henry's Commentary on the Whole Bible* commented on "the superlative excellency of the epistle" (363). In his *Commentary on the Epistle to the Romans,* Godet called Romans "the cathedral of the Christian faith" (1). *St. Paul's Epistle to the Romans* asserts, "The thorough study of the Epistle is really a theological education in itself" (*Griffith Thomas,* 24). In fact, Romans is the grand dynamic of true Christianity, as it includes first believing, then doing.

Appendix 2
OUTLINE

One approach to study Romans is by following this simple outline:

A. Righteousness required for sinful men
(Romans 1.16-3.20)

B. Righteousness provided through Jesus Christ
(Romans 3.21-26)

C. Righteousness received by faith in Jesus Christ
(Romans 3.27-4.25)

D. Righteousness experienced in this life
(Romans 5.1-8.39)

E. Righteousness and God's promise to Israel
(Romans 9-11)

F. Righteousness practically manifested in daily life
(Romans 12-16)

Appendix 3
THE ROMANS "TREE OF SALVATION"

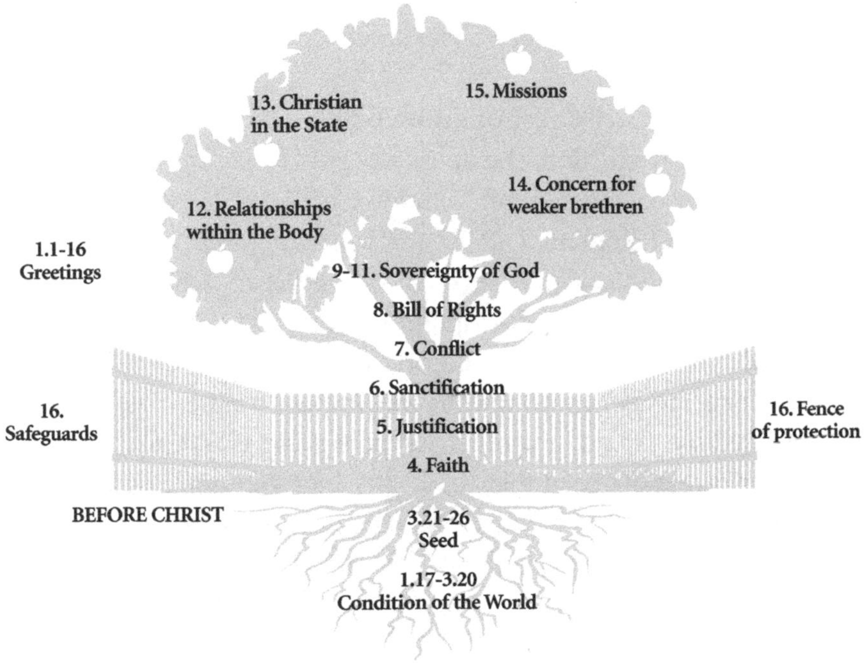

Chapter 1.1-16	Salutation
Chapter 1.18-32	"Gross" Sinners
Chapter 2.1-16	"Good" Sinners
Chapter 2.17-29	"Religious" Sinners
Chapter 3.21-26	God's Seed of Righteousness
Chapter 4	Faith
Chapter 5	Justification
Chapter 6	Sanctification
Chapter 7	Conflict
Chapter 8	Bill of Rights of the Believer
Chapters 9-11	Sovereignty of God
Chapters 12-15	Fruits
Chapter 16	Fence to Protect the Tree

Romans 1.1-16 Greetings

Romans 1.1-16 serves as the book's salutation. In it Paul addresses various groups. First, Paul identifies himself as a servant. Next, he identifies the Son of God, Jesus Christ. Third, he identifies his immediate audience—the beloved of God living in Rome. Fourth, he identifies the extent of a wider audience—all sinners.

Romans 1.17-3.20 Our Condition Before Christ

After the introduction, the apostle begins to lay the foundation to describe our condition without Christ in the world scene. This scene in Romans 1.17-3.20 is so frightening that it should motivate the most timid personal evangelist to action. Romans 1.18-3.20 paints a dire description of our condition before Jesus Christ's purchased salvation becomes our own.

There are some who may never have gone out and fallen into the mud of drugs or any other visible sins, so you think that you have never really been that "bad." Because you don't know how bad you were, you don't know how good you can be! You do not see the need for the gracious gift of our nail-scarred Savior.

Many of us do not fully understand the depths from which we came; thus, we do not fully comprehend what Christ has done for us. The apostle starts by making sure the revelation of our depravity is as dark as a moonless night. Then, against this dark background, he declares what the light of Jesus Christ has gloriously, legally done for us. This is a fact, not an emotion. Emotions follow facts, and our salvation is a factual legal transaction.

Romans 3.21-26 God's Seed of Righteousness

From Romans 1.18-3.20 we learn of the condition everyone was in before Jesus Christ justified us. He redeemed mankind instead of destroying them. In order to do this, He sent a Seed of righteousness into that same slimy, filthy, murky, and dirty world. Though God planted the first Adam in a beautiful garden according to Genesis 2.15, He planted the "last Adam" Jesus Christ into the filth of this world (Romans 3.21-26).

The Seed of righteousness I am talking about is the potent, powerful Seed. All people are now able to enjoy the power and benefits of what was accomplished by the planting of the Seed—Jesus.

This Seed is righteous. The main word in Romans is "righteousness," which means "right standing" or "rightness." From Romans 1.18-3.20 we learn that sinful man is not righteous. There is too much evidence against him. From verses 3.21-26 we see that God provided the necessary righteousness. The tree of righteousness continues to grow throughout the book. The righteous tree trunk grows by faith according to verses 3.27-4.25. From Romans 5.1-8.39 we see righteous branches produced in this life. Chapters 9 through 11 reveal the righteousness and the sovereignty of God. Finally, the fruit of righteousness is manifested in everyday life according to Romans, chapters 12 through 15, with chapter 16 concluding the whole righteous theme.

The Righteousness Seed Revealed Apart from the Law

Praise the Lord the Law has nothing to do with my salvation. All of these many things we have endeavored to do or to avoid in our lives avail nothing in our purchased salvation. I have moved, through the blood of Jesus Christ, into the kingdom of light. My "goodness" is the fruit of my salvation, not my effort to purchase salvation.

Spiritual Growth: Root vs. Fruit

How do the things you do every day, such as read your Bible, pray, witness and give an offering, earn your salvation? Are these things part of the root of your salvation, or are they are part of the fruit of your salvation? All of these righteous deeds, according to Romans, are a part of your fruit. The righteousness revealed in Romans is apart from any human efforts you do or do not do. Even the fine print of the Gospel reads that it is free. There is no trick. There is just a declaration that you are legally "free." This truth must get through to all of us who believe. Jesus Christ is the Seed. This Seed grows a big tree, with many branches and much fruit on it.

Romans 4: Faith

The roots of the tree are made strong by faith. Romans chapter 4 is to Romans what Hebrews 11 is to Hebrews. The faith chapter of Romans is chapter 4 where we read the account of Abraham. He is the father of faith and we learn how he came into this righteous relationship with God. How? He did it by faith. The Bible says he believed and it was counted to him as righteousness.

The time between when Abraham believed and when Abraham was circumcised is an important time span for mankind's freedom. If he had been justified at the time he received circumcision, the badge of identity, then he actually would have done something to earn his righteousness. He was declared justified with God when he believed—prior to any works.

Romans 5: Justification

Chapter 5 deals with our justification. By faith, we have been justified. The order is faith and justification lead to obedience. Our justification is a state of being declared by our righteous God. Our obedience is the fruit of our faith.

Romans 6: Sanctification

Chapter 6 is about our sanctification. The Righteous Seed that was planted in this sin-sick world continues to grow. It becomes fruitful when I allow it to work in me by faith. No matter what happens, I know that if I continue to believe, change will finally come. Your believing opens you up to receive His finished work.

YOUR BELIEVING OPENS YOU UP TO RECEIVE HIS FINISHED WORK.

Romans 7: A Conflict

Chapter 7 presents a number of conflicts. The chapter begins with the analogy of a marriage. The chapter is really about a deep conflict between grace and Law. The things I want to do, I cannot do.

The things I don't want to do, I keep doing over and over again. This conflict affects every believer. It is the believer, not the unbeliever who is involved in this conflict. In fact, this conflict describes the believer who has not fully internalized and believed Romans chapters 4 through 6 as his or her own full revelation. This conflicted believer bases his or her salvation on a feeling, rather than on a judicial legal, coming-down-of-the-gavel, which declared, "You are justified." Christ's sacrifice and atonement is more than sufficient to take away your sins and declare you righteous.

Romans 8: Bill of Rights of the Believer

As the Holy Spirit flows into the tree's new buds, He releases each into a unique calling. Chapter 8 is what I call the "Bill of Rights of the Believer." When you come to God, you must learn how to stand before the world and know what your rights are as a believer. What are your rights? Chapter 8 opens with no condemnation and ends with no separation. Throughout the whole chapter we see the Spirit enables us to walk free of condemnation. The weakness in our flesh is unable to do what God commands. God's power flowing through each believer is able to produce by faith the luscious fruit of the Spirit.

Romans 9-11: Sovereignty of God

Chapters 9 through 11 deal with the sovereignty of God and His covenant with Israel. God's plans are God's plans. He made a promise to Abraham—"I will bless you and your descendents"—and He intends to fulfill His promise naturally and spiritually.

Romans 12: Free to Serve God

Chapter 12 begins the fruit of chapters 12 through 15. Because you have been set free by His divine declaration, you are now ready to serve God in a new and a precious way. Chapter 12 provides the service guidelines and gifts, which operate out of divine fruit.

Romans 13: Obeying Civil Authority

Chapter 13 deals with the Christian and the state or the civil government. Chapter 13 tells us to obey those who have authority over us. For instance, the policeman in his position is serving God.

Romans 14: Relationships within the Family of God

Chapter 14 deals with relationships within the Body of Christ between the weaker and stronger brethren. This is another fruit, not a root chapter that commands the stronger not to offend the weaker!

Romans 15: Evangelism and Missions

Chapter 15, verse 1b, states, "We ought to help carry the doubts and qualms of others—and not to please ourselves." Verse 3 gives the reason why: "For Christ (gave no thought to His own interests) to please Himself . . . " I have titled chapter 15 as "Missions" because some eleven times in this chapter, the author talks about the Gentiles coming to know Christ. The book of Revelation reminds us that the leaves and the fruit of the tree are for "the healing of the nations" (see Rev. 22.2).

Romans 16: Safeguard

Finally, the last chapter, 16, I have titled the fence that provides a safeguard for the tree. Here we are told to mark those who cause divisions and those who flatter. Avoid them. The root has been planted, the tree has grown, now, at the end of the book of Romans, a strong fence of relationships must be built around the tree for protection.

As you can see from the tree diagram, the revelation contained from chapter 4 to chapter 8 is the root and the trunk of our salvation. These chapters reveal to us that our salvation is on the basis of His strength, not ours. We are unable to successfully move into chapters 12 through 15 without first possessing the root of chapters 4 through 8. In chapter 5 we learn we died with Christ to our flesh. In chapter 6, that we are baptized into His death. In chapter 7, we learn we are now joined to a new, living partner. In chapter 8, we are now free! We are ready to "... present your bodies a living sacrifice, holy, acceptable unto God, which is your reasonable service" (Rom. 12.1).

Believers are trying to do chapters 12 through 15 without the root of chapters 4 through 8. Life flows from the root, not from the fruit. Divine energy comes from uniting with Christ's work that was accomplished on Calvary. This is the source of our strength. It flows from root upward to the fruit.

Remember, there are roots and there are fruits. In our roots we die with Christ. In our fruit we live with Christ in the power of the upper room. The roots represent our death in Christ, and the fruit represents the impartation of divine life. We live on a beaten path between Calvary and the upper room—between root and fruit.

After reading Romans chapters 12 through 15, you may perceive yourself as not measuring up to such high standards. By the grace of God, stop trying to measure up! Focus on Him and believe. Relax. You are either in Christ, or you are not. When you are in Christ, the Spirit will bear witness in your life. Abide in the vine and produce fruit. Let us all be strong in root, in trunk, and branches and let the fruit blossom forth sweet to the nations.

WORKS CONSULTED

Baxter, Ern. Compilation of notes.

Godet, F. *Commentary on the Epistle to the Romans.*
Grand Rapids: Zondervan Publishing House, 1970.

Gothard, Bill. Basic Youth Conflicts.

Henry, Matthew. *Matthew Henry's Commentary on the Whole Bible.*
Vol. VI. New York: Fleming H. Revell Company, (reprint).

Luther, Martin. *Commentary on Romans.*
Grand Rapids: Kregel Publications, 1976.

Peterson, Eugene H. *The Message.*
Colorado Springs: Navpress, 2003.

The Modern Language Bible. The Berkeley Version. Revised Edition.
Grand Rapids: Zondervan Publishing House, 1969.

Moffatt, James A.R. *The Bible, A New Translation.*
New York: Harper & Brothers Publishers, 1950.

New Testament, Revised Standard Version.
New York: Nelson & Sons, 1946.

Thomas, W.H. Griffith. *St. Paul's Epistle to the Romans: A Devotional Commentary.*
Grand Rapids: Wm. B. Eerdmans Publishing Company, 1972.

Weymouth, Richard Francis. *The New Testament in Modern Speech.*
New York: Harper & Brothers, Publishers, 1929.

Printed in the USA
CPSIA information can be obtained
at www.ICGtesting.com
JSHW022215140824
68134JS00018B/1067

9 781614 483700